Mastering AWS IAM
Troubleshooting and Solutions

Table of Contents

Part 1: Getting Started with IAM

Chapter 1: Introduction to AWS IAM

A Comprehensive Introduction to AWS IAM: Secure Access Control in the Cloud

When it comes to securing your AWS environment, one of the most critical services at your disposal is **AWS Identity and Access Management (IAM)**. This powerful, centralized service helps you define who can access which resources, and under what conditions they can do so. By understanding its core features and concepts, you can enforce best-practice security standards, maintain compliance, and ensure that everyone—from developers to end-users—interacts with your cloud environment in a controlled and traceable manner.

What is AWS IAM?

AWS Identity and Access Management (IAM) is a web service that enables you to manage access to AWS resources securely. At its core, IAM addresses two fundamental questions:

1. **Who can access your resources?** (Authentication)
2. **What actions can they perform?** (Authorization)

By managing these elements centrally, IAM provides a strong foundation for maintaining security, governance, and compliance across your entire AWS infrastructure.

Key IAM Features

1. Centralized Access Management:
IAM simplifies identity and access management by giving you a single control panel for configuring permissions and policies. You can manage users across multiple AWS accounts, use roles to delegate access, and streamline permissions to meet organizational requirements.

2. Granular Permissions:

IAM encourages the principle of least privilege, allowing you to grant the minimal level of access needed to complete a specific task. Policies can be further refined using conditions—such as time-based or IP-based restrictions—ensuring that permissions are both minimal and context-aware.

3. Temporary Security Credentials:

To mitigate risks associated with long-term credentials, IAM integrates with the AWS Security Token Service (STS). This makes it simple to issue temporary, short-lived credentials for users or external partners. Federated access via SAML or OpenID Connect can also be leveraged for short-term, trusted collaborations without directly sharing long-term keys.

4. Flexible Identity Options:

With IAM, you can manage **Users** and **Groups** to control access for individuals and teams. Additionally, **Roles** allow services or external entities to assume permissions without requiring fixed credentials. This flexibility is crucial for enabling secure, dynamic workflows.

5. Advanced Policy Management:

AWS provides **Managed Policies**—ready-made policies maintained by AWS for common scenarios. You can also define **Customer-Managed Policies** tailored to your specific needs. The **Policy Simulator** tool lets you test policies before implementing them, ensuring that each permission set does what you intend.

6. Audit and Compliance Tools:

For visibility and compliance, tools like **IAM Access Analyzer** and **AWS CloudTrail** help you track changes, identify overly permissive access, and monitor user activity. These auditing capabilities ensure you maintain a robust security posture and meet regulatory standards.

Core IAM Concepts

1. IAM Users:
A user in IAM represents a single individual or application that requires access to AWS. Each user has their own credentials and can be granted permissions through policies. For example, a developer who needs to interact with certain S3 buckets can have user-specific policies attached.

2. IAM Groups:
Groups simplify permission management by bundling multiple users together. Assigning a policy to a group automatically applies those permissions to all group members. For instance, a "Developers" group might have broad access to development resources but not production ones.

3. IAM Roles:
Roles are like "permission containers" that can be assumed temporarily by users, applications, or AWS services. Common use cases include allowing an EC2 instance to interact with S3 on your behalf (a service role) or enabling trusted partners from another account to securely access your resources (a cross-account role).

4. Policies:
Policies are JSON documents that define permissions. They specify **Effect** (Allow or Deny), **Actions** (like s3:ListBucket), **Resources** (such as a particular S3 bucket), and **Conditions** (like time of day). There are three types of policies:

- **AWS-Managed Policies:** Predefined by AWS.
- **Customer-Managed Policies:** Created and maintained by you.
- **Inline Policies:** Embedded directly into a single user, group, or role.

5. Permissions and Their Behavior:
Permissions are granted by attaching policies to identities. Notably, IAM uses a "deny by default" model, meaning actions

are not allowed unless explicitly permitted. And if a resource policy ever includes an explicit "Deny," that will override any "Allow" you've set.

Bringing It All Together

AWS IAM lies at the heart of a secure, scalable cloud environment. By defining users, groups, roles, and policies, you create a finely tuned system of identity and access control. Leveraging IAM's centralized management, advanced policy features, and compliance tools, you can confidently implement least-privilege access, minimize risk, and maintain a strong security posture.

Whether you're just getting started in AWS or already scaling complex cloud architectures, understanding IAM is a crucial step toward building a safe, compliant, and well-governed AWS infrastructure.

Maximizing Security and Efficiency with AWS IAM: Centralized Control and Multi-Account Management

When managing a growing cloud environment, ensuring that the right people have the right level of access to the right resources—without unnecessary complexity—is a top priority. **AWS Identity and Access Management (IAM)** streamlines this process, offering powerful tools for centralized access control and secure multi-account management. By leveraging IAM's robust feature set, you can strengthen your security posture, maintain compliance, and reduce administrative overhead as your AWS footprint scales.

Centralized Access Control: One Place to Manage It All

At the heart of IAM is the ability to manage who can do what across all of your AWS services and resources, all from a single control plane. Instead of juggling multiple fragmented permission sets, IAM allows you to create and apply consistent, reusable policies throughout your environment, ensuring both flexibility and uniformity.

Key Features:

- **Unified Access Policies:**
  Rather than maintaining separate permission sets for each service, centralize all your access configurations. For example, you could apply one read-only policy to every S3 bucket used by a particular team, streamlining permissions management.
- **Granular Permissions:**
  IAM lets you define permissions at a fine-grained level. This approach ensures you grant only the minimum required access—following the principle of least privilege. You might allow a particular user group the s3:GetObject action on a single bucket, ensuring they can only read content from that specific resource.
- **Audit and Monitoring:**
  Integration with AWS CloudTrail allows you to track changes to IAM roles, policies, and user activity over time. These detailed logs make it easier to spot unusual behavior, troubleshoot permissions issues, and meet compliance requirements.
- **Policy Reusability:**
  IAM's managed and customer-managed policies let you reuse permission sets across users, groups, and roles, minimizing repetitive work and reducing the risk of errors. Pre-configured AWS-managed policies also simplify setup by providing best-practice templates for common use cases.

Centralized Control Benefits:

- **Efficiency:** Manage all your permissions in one place, reducing complexity and administrative overhead.
- **Consistency:** Apply uniform security standards across services, ensuring that every resource adheres to the same set of policies.

- **Scalability:** Easily adapt as your organization grows, adding new users, services, and resources without losing your security posture.
- **Security:** Keep misconfigurations at bay by ensuring all policies are created, applied, and reviewed from a single, controlled location.

Secure Multi-Account Management: Balancing Isolation with Accessibility

Organizations frequently operate multiple AWS accounts to maintain strict isolation, align resources with departments, or implement sandbox environments for testing. IAM provides a robust framework for managing access across these accounts without sacrificing security or ease of administration.

Key Features:

- **AWS Organizations:**
  Organize multiple AWS accounts into a hierarchical structure of Organizational Units (OUs). Apply Service Control Policies (SCPs) to set permission boundaries and maintain compliance across entire groups of accounts.
- **Cross-Account Roles:**
  Grant users or AWS services in one account controlled access to resources in another—without sharing long-term credentials. For example, your development team in Account A can assume a role that lets them deploy applications to a production environment in Account B.
- **Permissions Guardrails:**
  Use SCPs to set non-negotiable guardrails—like preventing public S3 buckets—across all accounts in your organization. These guardrails ensure consistency, help maintain compliance, and reduce the risk of accidental exposure.
- **IAM Identity Center (Formerly AWS SSO):**
  Centrally manage workforce access across multiple AWS accounts and applications. By integrating IAM

Identity Center with IAM roles, you can simplify access management, provide single sign-on capabilities, and make it easier for users to navigate your multi-account environment.

Multi-Account Management Benefits:

- **Isolation:** By design, separate accounts limit the blast radius of security incidents and ensure compliance boundaries for different departments or projects.
- **Delegation:** Cross-account roles and centralized controls let you grant secure access without sharing keys or logging into multiple accounts.
- **Governance:** Establish consistent policies and security guardrails at scale, meeting organizational and regulatory requirements more easily.
- **Scalability:** As your organization adds more accounts and services, a multi-account strategy with IAM provides the flexibility to manage complex setups efficiently.

Driving Security and Growth with IAM

By employing AWS IAM for centralized access control and multi-account management, you not only enhance your security stance but also streamline day-to-day operations. From applying uniform policies across resources to securely delegating cross-account access, IAM ensures that as you grow, you do so with confidence, agility, and regulatory peace of mind.

In essence, IAM's robust feature set empowers you to maintain strong security boundaries, scale securely, and keep your cloud environment well-organized—no matter how complex or dynamic it becomes. For any AWS user looking to enforce consistent security practices and simplify resource administration, IAM stands as an indispensable tool.

Getting Started with Key IAM Terminologies: Users, Groups, Roles, and Policies

When it comes to securing your AWS environment, **AWS Identity and Access Management (IAM)** provides the foundational building blocks. At the core of IAM are a few crucial concepts—**users, groups, roles, and policies**—that together define who can access your AWS resources, what they can do, and under what conditions. Understanding these terms is key to implementing a well-structured, scalable, and secure access control system.

Users and Groups

IAM Users:
An IAM user represents a person or a machine that directly interacts with AWS. Each user has their own credentials—like usernames, passwords, and access keys—for signing in to the AWS Management Console or making API calls. By default, new IAM users have no permissions; you grant them the necessary privileges via policies. For instance, a developer might need read and write access to specific Amazon S3 buckets, or permissions to spin up new Amazon EC2 instances.

IAM Groups:
Groups are collections of users, allowing you to manage permissions for multiple users simultaneously. Instead of assigning policies user by user, you attach them once to a group—like "Developers" or "Admins"—and everyone in that group inherits those permissions. This approach streamlines administration and ensures consistent access privileges across teams.

When to Use:

- **Users:** Ideal for individuals needing ongoing access to AWS resources, such as members of your development team.

- **Groups:** Perfect for standardizing permissions for entire teams or departments without having to manage each user's permissions separately.

Roles

IAM Roles:
Unlike users, roles don't have long-term credentials. Instead, a role defines a set of permissions that can be temporarily assumed by a user, an application, or even an AWS service. When something assumes a role, AWS Security Token Service (STS) issues short-term credentials, enabling secure, time-limited access.

Use Cases for Roles:

- **Service Roles:** Let AWS services like Amazon EC2 or AWS Lambda interact with other services (e.g., accessing an S3 bucket) without sharing permanent credentials.
- **Cross-Account Access:** Allow trusted users or applications from one AWS account to securely operate resources in another account.
- **Federated Roles:** Grant external users who authenticate through SAML or OpenID Connect temporary access to AWS resources, without creating dedicated IAM users for them.

When to Use:

- **Roles:** Whenever you need temporary, just-in-time access without distributing permanent credentials. They're perfect for short-lived tasks, automated workflows, and external integrations.

Policies and Permissions

IAM Policies:
Policies are JSON documents that describe which actions are

allowed or denied on which resources. They specify the **Effect** (Allow or Deny), **Action** (e.g., s3:ListBucket), **Resource** (like a particular S3 bucket), and optional **Conditions** (such as time-based or IP-based restrictions).

Types of Policies:

- **AWS-Managed Policies:** Predefined and maintained by AWS. Ideal for common scenarios like granting read-only access to S3.
- **Customer-Managed Policies:** Custom policies you create to fit your organization's unique requirements.
- **Inline Policies:** Embedded directly into a single IAM user, group, or role, usually for very specific, fine-tuned permissions.

IAM Permissions:
Permissions are what you ultimately grant to identities. By default, everything is denied. You must explicitly allow actions through policies. And if any policy explicitly denies something, that denial always takes precedence.

When to Use:

- **Policies:** Whenever you want to set or refine the allowed actions for a user, group, or role. Policies form the backbone of your security strategy, enforcing the principle of least privilege and ensuring each identity has only the access it needs.

Putting It All Together

By combining users, groups, roles, and policies, you create a secure and manageable system of access control:

- **Users & Groups** help you define identities—real people or applications—and assign them baseline permissions in a scalable way.

- **Roles** handle temporary scenarios, enabling AWS services, external partners, or cross-account resources to perform tasks without sharing permanent credentials.
- **Policies** and **Permissions** dictate exactly what each identity can (and can't) do, providing the fine-grained control needed for a robust security posture.

As your AWS environment evolves, a solid understanding of these IAM terminologies ensures that you can grow securely and confidently. By carefully crafting who has access, what they can do, and under what circumstances, you'll maintain a resilient and compliant cloud infrastructure that's ready to scale with your organization's needs.

Summary of Chapter 1: Introduction to AWS IAM

In Chapter 1, we explored the foundational concepts and benefits of AWS Identity and Access Management (IAM). We began by understanding what IAM is—a centralized, secure way to manage who can access AWS resources and what they can do with them. We then covered the key advantages IAM brings to cloud environments, including centralized access control and secure multi-account management, both of which simplify governance and promote a strong security posture.

Next, we delved into the core IAM terminologies—users, groups, roles, and policies—and how they work together. Users and groups provide a structured way to grant permissions to individuals and teams, while roles enable temporary, situation-specific access without distributing long-term credentials. Policies, expressed as JSON documents, precisely define allowed or denied actions, ensuring that every entity has only the permissions it requires.

In essence, Chapter 1 established the foundation for understanding IAM's core features, benefits, and building blocks. It laid the groundwork for applying these concepts to create a secure, scalable, and well-governed AWS environment.

Chapter 2: Setting Up IAM

How to Securely Set Up Your AWS Account from Day One

When you're just getting started with Amazon Web Services (AWS), it's easy to jump straight into provisioning resources and exploring services. But before you spin up your first EC2 instance or store a single object in S3, take a moment to establish a strong security foundation. Two key steps in the initial setup process—securing your root user and adding alternate contact details—will help ensure that you're protecting your environment from the very start.

Secure Your AWS Root User

Your AWS root user is the single most powerful entity in your account. It holds full administrative privileges and can do just about anything, from modifying billing information to deleting entire infrastructures. With that level of control comes increased responsibility: if your root user credentials are compromised, it can lead to catastrophic consequences. Here's how to lock it down.

Enable Multi-Factor Authentication (MFA)

MFA adds a crucial second layer of protection. Instead of just a password, anyone logging in as the root user needs a one-time code from an MFA device (such as a virtual MFA app or a hardware security key).

How to set it up:

1. Sign in as the root user.
2. Go to **IAM Dashboard → Security Credentials**.
3. Under **Multi-Factor Authentication (MFA),** click **Activate MFA**.

4. Choose your MFA device (e.g., an authenticator app or a hardware token).
5. Follow the on-screen prompts to pair and test your device.

Use a Strong, Unique Password

Resist the urge to reuse old passwords. Set a unique password that's at least 12 characters long and includes a mix of uppercase, lowercase, numbers, and symbols. Consider using a password manager to store it securely.

Don't Use the Root User for Daily Tasks

Only use the root user for tasks that strictly require it—like managing billing or establishing Organization-level settings. For everyday operations, create IAM users or roles with just enough permission for the job at hand.

Monitor Root User Access

Track who's doing what with your root user credentials. Enable AWS CloudTrail for detailed access logs, and consider setting up CloudWatch alarms to trigger alerts whenever the root user is used.

Best Practices:

- Delete any root access keys that may have been created during your initial setup.
- Store credentials in a secure location (like a password manager).
- Regularly review and update your account's security configuration.

Add Alternate Contact Details

In addition to securing your account, make sure AWS knows how to reach you (or someone on your team) when it matters most. Providing alternate contacts ensures you won't miss critical notifications—like security alerts, billing issues, or important operational updates.

How to Add Alternate Contacts

1. Sign in to the AWS Management Console as the root user or an IAM user with the necessary permissions.
2. Head to the **Billing and Cost Management Dashboard** and select **Account Settings**.
3. Under the relevant sections, enter details for:
   o **Alternate Billing Contact:** Someone responsible for financial inquiries.
   o **Alternate Security Contact:** A person (or team) ready to respond to security issues.
   o **Alternate Operations Contact:** An individual who can handle operational updates, like service outages or maintenance notices.
4. Verify the information and save your changes.

Best Practices:

- Choose contacts who regularly check their email or phone messages.
- Use role-based email addresses (e.g., security@company.com) to ensure continuity if staff changes occur.
- Update these details promptly when personnel or responsibilities shift.

Building a Strong Foundation

Securing your root user and setting up alternate contact details might seem like small administrative chores. But these early steps lay the groundwork for a resilient AWS environment. By enforcing MFA, using strong passwords, avoiding routine root user actions, and monitoring access, you protect your account from the get-go. Meanwhile, keeping your alternate contacts current ensures that you're always in the loop, ready to act quickly if something demands your immediate attention.

Your journey with AWS has just begun. Start on the right foot by prioritizing security and communication. The few minutes you spend now can save you countless headaches down the road.

Streamlining Access with IAM Users and Groups in AWS

When you're building out your AWS environment, one of your earliest tasks should be defining *who* can access your resources and *how*. AWS Identity and Access Management (IAM) provides the structure you need: you create individual identities called IAM users, then organize them into IAM groups to streamline permissions management. By doing this, you'll reduce the complexity of assigning privileges user-by-user and ensure a consistent, secure foundation for your growing cloud infrastructure.

Step-by-Step Guide: Creating IAM Users

What is an IAM User?
An IAM user is a single entity—like a developer, system administrator, or application—that interacts directly with AWS. Each user has credentials (like passwords and access keys) and assigned permissions that determine what actions they can take.

How to Add an IAM User:

1. **Sign In:**
   Log in to the AWS Management Console with administrative credentials.
2. **Access IAM:**
   From the AWS console homepage, open the IAM service.
3. **Add a New User:**
   In the IAM dashboard, select **Users** from the left-hand menu, then click **Add Users**.
4. **Set User Details:**

- o **User Name:** Choose a unique identifier (e.g., jane_developer).
- o **Access Type:**
  - **Management Console Access:** For users who need to log into the AWS console.
  - **Programmatic Access:** For users who interact with AWS via CLI, SDKs, or APIs.
5. If you enable console access, set a custom password or let AWS generate one.
6. **Assign Permissions:**
   Choose one of three methods:
   - o **Add User to Group:** Let the user inherit policies from a group.
   - o **Attach Existing Policies Directly:** Assign AWS-managed or custom policies right to the user.
   - o **Copy Permissions from Another User:** Duplicate configurations from an existing user.
7. **Optional Tags:**
   Add metadata (e.g., department or project) to help organize and filter users later.
8. **Review & Create:**
   Check all details and permissions, then click **Create User**. If you enabled programmatic access, AWS provides access keys—store these securely.
9. **Securely Distribute Credentials:**
   Provide the user's login details (URL, username, password/access keys) through a secure channel (like a password manager).

Best Practices for IAM Users:

- • **Enforce Strong Passwords:**
  Use complex passwords and consider rotating them regularly.

- **Minimize Access Keys:**
  Only create access keys if absolutely necessary, and rotate them frequently.
- **Audit Regularly:**
  Identify unused accounts and disable them to reduce the attack surface.

Simplifying Management with IAM Groups

What Are IAM Groups?
Think of groups as "permission buckets" that several users can share. Instead of granting the same policy to every developer individually, place all developers in a "Developers" group that has the necessary permissions. This centralizes policy management and saves time.

How to Create an IAM Group:

1. **Access IAM:**
   In the IAM dashboard, select **Groups** from the left-hand menu, then click **Create Group**.
2. **Name the Group:**
   Use something clear and descriptive, such as Developers or AppSupportTeam.
3. **Attach Policies:**
   Add one or more policies—AWS-managed or custom— to define the group's permissions. For example, a group called Developers might have AmazonS3ReadOnlyAccess.
4. **Add Users (Optional):**
   Immediately assign users to the group, or add them later. Users inherit the group's policies instantly.
5. **Review & Create:**
   Check your configuration, then create the group.

Adding Users to a Group:

- Go to the **Users** section in IAM.
- Select the user(s) you want to add.

- Click **Add to Groups**, choose the group, and save.

Why Use IAM Groups?

- **Easier Permission Management:**
  Update the group policy once, and all members get the changes.
- **Organizational Clarity:**
  Group users by roles (e.g., Admins), departments (e.g., Finance), or projects.
- **Consistent Access:**
  Every developer in the Developers group shares the same baseline permissions, reducing the risk of accidental misconfiguration.

Example:
Let's say you have five developers who need read-only access to S3 buckets. Instead of attaching the AmazonS3ReadOnlyAccess policy to each developer, you:

1. Create a group called Developers.
2. Attach AmazonS3ReadOnlyAccess to that group.
3. Add all five developers to the Developers group.

Now they all have uniform, read-only S3 permissions without any extra effort.

Building a Secure, Scalable Foundation

By strategically creating IAM users and grouping them together, you can manage access efficiently as your AWS environment grows. IAM groups let you grant and modify permissions once, knowing that every member of that group will have the correct, up-to-date privileges. Together, IAM users and groups form a critical piece of your overall security strategy in AWS.

In essence, the approach is simple: define individual users, collect them into logical groups, and manage their permissions centrally. This foundational setup not only streamlines administration but also reduces the risk of errors and ensures a consistent, secure approach to identity and access management across your entire organization.

Get to Know the IAM Dashboard: Your Central Hub for Access Management in AWS

When it comes to managing identity and access within your AWS environment, the **IAM Dashboard** is your go-to control center. From overseeing user accounts and groups to auditing credentials and refining policies, the dashboard centralizes all the moving parts of your cloud security. Understanding how to navigate and leverage its tools can greatly simplify your day-to-day administration and enhance your overall security posture.

Key Features at a Glance

The IAM Dashboard is more than just a landing page. It's a command center that surfaces key security insights and provides easy navigation to critical IAM components:

1. **Security Status**
   Start here to assess your account's overall security posture. The dashboard recommends best practices, such as enabling MFA on the root account and avoiding the use of root access keys for daily tasks. Consider it your security checklist, ensuring you're taking the right steps from the get-go.
2. **Easy Access to IAM Resources**
   With just a few clicks, you can manage all core IAM building blocks:
   o **Users:** Create, manage, and configure login credentials and MFA for each user.
   o **Groups:** Bundle users together by role or department, making it simpler to assign and manage permissions.
   o **Roles:** Grant temporary access to services or users without sharing long-term credentials.

- **Policies:** Define who can do what, down to the finest detail. Apply policies to users, groups, or roles to ensure consistent permissions.

3. **Policy Simulator**
   Unsure if a newly crafted policy does what you intend? Use the built-in Policy Simulator to test requests and confirm that you're allowing (or denying) the correct actions—before pushing changes to production.

4. **Credential Reports**
   Stay on top of your users' access keys, passwords, and MFA usage. Credential Reports help you spot stale credentials, unused accounts, or missing MFA, ensuring you can remediate security gaps early.

5. **Identity Center Integration**
   Formerly known as AWS SSO, Identity Center helps you manage user access across multiple AWS accounts and even external applications—all from a single interface. This integration turns the IAM Dashboard into a one-stop shop for broader organizational access management.

6. **Access Analyzer**
   Access Analyzer is a powerful feature that highlights resources shared outside your AWS account. It analyzes policies, identifies overly permissive permissions, and offers insights to refine your security boundaries.

Navigating the IAM Dashboard Efficiently

The IAM Dashboard's intuitive layout and handy shortcuts help you move quickly between tasks and uncover key insights.

1. **Use the Breadcrumbs**
   Navigating between pages is a breeze with the breadcrumb trail at the top. For example, if you're deep into a user's details, you can jump back to the Users list with a single click.

2. **Leverage the Sidebar**
   The left-hand menu puts core actions front and center:
   - **Dashboard:** A quick security snapshot.

     o **Users, Groups, Roles:** Fast access to identity management tools.

     o **Policies:** Your one-stop policy repository.

3. **Search and Filter**
   With the search bar at the top, you can locate users, groups, roles, or policies by keyword. Add filters by tags, access key status, or permissions to quickly zero in on exactly what you need.

4. **Tagging for Organization**
   Add custom tags (like Department:Finance or Project:DataAnalytics) to users, groups, and policies. These tags make it easier to categorize identities and resources, so you can filter and manage them efficiently.

5. **Generate On-Demand Reports**
   Run Credential Reports to detect potential security issues at a glance. Find out which users lack MFA or which have access keys that haven't been used for months—insights that help you maintain a vigilant security stance.

6. **In-Console Documentation Links**
   Stuck or need a quick refresher? The dashboard includes documentation links right where you need them, so you can consult AWS best practices without leaving the console.

7. **CLI and API Integration**
   The dashboard is also a great learning tool. By understanding how resources are organized here, you can better plan your command-line scripts and API calls later—perfect for automating routine tasks and scaling your environment.

Example: Checking MFA Compliance

Let's say you want to ensure every user in your account is using MFA:

1. **Start at the Dashboard:** Check the Security Status to see if MFA is enabled on the root user and gauge overall compliance.

2. **Go to Users:** Click on "Users" in the sidebar to view all accounts.
3. **Filter or Search:** Use filters to isolate users without MFA.
4. **Update MFA Settings:** Select a user, configure their MFA, and repeat as needed until everyone meets your MFA requirement.

Building a Secure, Manageable IAM Framework

The IAM Dashboard is more than just a tool—it's the command center that ties together your entire identity and access control strategy. By mastering its features and navigation shortcuts, you'll set a strong, scalable security foundation for your AWS environment. With real-time insights, easy-to-use configuration tools, and built-in best practice guidelines, the IAM Dashboard empowers you to confidently manage access across your cloud infrastructure.

Strengthening Your AWS Security with Customizable Password Policies

Passwords remain a critical line of defense in any security strategy. As organizations increasingly rely on the cloud, enforcing robust password policies helps maintain a secure AWS environment. With AWS Identity and Access Management (IAM), you can tailor password complexity requirements and rotation schedules to meet your organization's security standards—ultimately reducing the risk of unauthorized access.

Why Password Policies Matter

Setting clear password policies ensures that your IAM users follow best practices when creating and maintaining their credentials. By enforcing rules around complexity and expiration, you encourage stronger passwords that are less susceptible to brute-force attacks or being compromised over time.

Defining Your Password Requirements

IAM's password policy features allow you to:

- **Set Complexity Rules:** Enforce a minimum length and require a mix of uppercase letters, lowercase letters, numbers, and special characters.
- **Prevent Reuse:** Limit how often users can recycle old passwords.
- **Control Expiration:** Set how long a password can remain active before it must be changed.

This flexibility lets you align your cloud security posture with internal policies and industry compliance standards.

Step-by-Step: Configuring Your Password Policy

1. **Sign In to the AWS Management Console:**
   Use an account with administrative privileges.
2. **Go to the IAM Dashboard:**
   From the console, select **IAM** to open the Identity and Access Management service.
3. **Access Account Settings:**
   In the left-hand navigation, choose **Account Settings**. Under **Password Policy**, click **Edit**.
4. **Define Complexity Requirements:**
   - **Length:** AWS recommends at least 8 characters, but consider a minimum of 12 for added security.
   - **Character Mix:** Require uppercase, lowercase, numbers, and special characters.
   - **Prevent Reuse:** Disallow the use of the last few passwords (e.g., the previous 5) to avoid repetition.
5. **Set Expiration and Rotation Schedules:**
   - **Expiration:** For instance, require a password change every 90 days.

- o **Early Changes:** Restrict users from changing passwords too frequently, preventing trivial rotations that weaken password security.
6. **Save Changes:**
   Confirm your settings. All IAM users must now comply with these policies during password creation and updates.

Example Policy:

- 12-character minimum length
- At least 1 uppercase letter, 1 lowercase letter, 1 number, and 1 special character
- Rotate passwords every 90 days
- Cannot reuse the last 5 passwords

Encouraging Regular Rotation

Regular password rotation helps mitigate the risk of compromised credentials remaining in use indefinitely. While too-frequent changes can lead users to choose weaker, easily guessable passwords, a balanced rotation schedule (e.g., every 90 days) maintains security without sacrificing usability.

How to Enforce Rotation:

- **Enable Password Expiration:** Set a maximum password age in your policy.
- **Educate Users:** Notify them about when their passwords will expire so they can prepare in advance.
- **Credential Reports:** Use the IAM Credential Reports feature to track compliance and identify users who are overdue for password changes.
- **Automate Notifications:** Consider using AWS Lambda and Amazon SNS to send email reminders to users as their password expiration date approaches.

Monitoring and Auditing Compliance

Security policies aren't "set-and-forget" tools. Regular monitoring ensures that users adhere to your standards and that your policies evolve alongside changing security landscapes.

- **Credential Reports:**
  Download and review reports to see when users last changed their passwords, who lacks MFA, and whether any accounts are dormant.
- **CloudTrail Logs:**
  AWS CloudTrail can log any changes to your password policies, giving you visibility into when and why alterations occur.
- **Integration with MFA:**
  For an additional layer of security, pair password policies with MFA. Even if a password is compromised, MFA requirements significantly reduce the risk of unauthorized access.

Real-World Example: Financial Institutions

Consider a financial institution that must meet stringent regulatory requirements. By setting:

- A 12-character minimum password length
- Required uppercase, lowercase, numeric, and special characters
- A 90-day expiration period
- Prohibitions on reusing the last 5 passwords

…they ensure that their user credentials meet strong security standards. Through credential reports, the security team can verify compliance regularly, and automated email alerts can prompt users to rotate their passwords before expiration. Combined with MFA, these measures offer comprehensive, layered protection.

Laying the Foundation for Stronger Security

Password policies are a foundational element of any robust identity and access management strategy. By customizing and enforcing complexity and rotation requirements, you harden your AWS environment against credential-based threats. When you integrate these policies with consistent monitoring, MFA, and clear communication to users, you create a resilient security posture that grows stronger over time.

In the cloud, proactive and well-defined password policies aren't just best practices—they're a critical step toward safeguarding the integrity and continuity of your business operations.

Chapter 3: Basic IAM Policies

A Practical Guide to IAM Policies: Fine-Grained Access Control in AWS

When it comes to securing your AWS environment, having a strong handle on who can access which resources—and under what conditions—is paramount. **IAM policies** form the cornerstone of this security model. These JSON documents control permissions by defining what actions specific identities (users, groups, or roles) can take on which resources, and even under which conditions.

In this post, we'll break down what IAM policies are, how they're structured, and how you can use them to implement fine-grained access controls that align with the principle of least privilege.

What Exactly Are IAM Policies?

At a high level, IAM policies are the rules of engagement for your AWS resources. They say: "This identity (like a user or role) can take this action (like listing or writing to an S3 bucket) on this resource (a particular S3 bucket or EC2 instance) under these conditions (for example, only if the request comes from a certain IP range or time period)." By defining these rules in JSON format, IAM policies give you a flexible, programmable way to manage access securely and precisely.

Understanding the Policy Structure

IAM policies are written in JSON, but don't worry—you don't need to be a coding guru. The structure is straightforward:

```
{
  "Version": "2012-10-17",
  "Statement": [
    {
      "Effect": "Allow",
      "Action": "s3:ListBucket",
      "Resource": "arn:aws:s3:::example-bucket"
    }
  ]
}
```

Key elements:

- **Version:** Specifies the policy language version. Always use the latest date ("2012-10-17") for maximum compatibility.
- **Statement:** A policy can contain one or more statements, each defining a specific permission rule.
- **Effect:** Determines whether the statement allows or denies access. ("Allow" or "Deny")
- **Action:** Lists the operations you're granting or denying. For example, s3:ListBucket gives permission to list the contents of a bucket.
- **Resource:** Identifies the AWS resource affected by the policy (using ARNs—Amazon Resource Names).
- **Condition (optional):** Adds further restrictions, such as time-based or IP-based limitations.

Breaking Down the Components

1. Actions:

Actions map directly to AWS API operations. For example, ec2:StartInstances allows the initiation of EC2 instances, while s3:PutObject permits uploading objects to an S3 bucket. You can use wildcards to grant broad permissions, such as "Action": "s3:*" to allow all S3 actions—just remember that broader permissions mean a bigger security risk.

2. Resources:

Resources specify which AWS asset the policy applies to. An S3 bucket might be arn:aws:s3:::example-bucket, or an EC2 instance might have an ARN like arn:aws:ec2:us-east-1:123456789012:instance/i-1234567890abcdef. Tightening the resource scope (e.g., a single bucket instead of all buckets) enforces the principle of least privilege.

3. Conditions:

Conditions let you add contextual checks. For example, you might allow a user to download files from S3 only if they're connecting from a certain IP range or only during business hours. Conditions look like this:

```
"Condition": {
  "IpAddress": {
    "aws:SourceIp": "203.0.113.0/24"
  }
}
```

A More Complex Example

Consider a policy that allows a user to get objects from a specific S3 bucket, but only if their request comes from a trusted IP range:

```
{
  "Version": "2012-10-17",
  "Statement": [
    {
      "Effect": "Allow",
      "Action": "s3:GetObject",
      "Resource": "arn:aws:s3:::example-bucket/*",
      "Condition": {
        "IpAddress": {
          "aws:SourceIp": "203.0.113.0/24"
        }
      }
    }
  ]
}
```

What's happening here?

- **Effect:** Allow means we're granting permission.
- **Action:** s3:GetObject lets the user download (read) objects.
- **Resource:** Applies to all objects in example-bucket.
- **Condition:** Limits downloads to requests from 203.0.113.0/24.

Best Practices for Writing IAM Policies

1. **Use the Principle of Least Privilege:**
    Only grant the minimum necessary permissions. If a user needs read-only access to a single S3 bucket, don't give them s3:* on all buckets.
2. **Be Specific:**
    Avoid Resource: "*" unless absolutely necessary. Narrowing scope reduces the risk of misuse.
3. **Test Your Policies:**
    Use the IAM Policy Simulator to confirm that your policies behave as intended before applying them.
4. **Leverage AWS-Managed Policies:**
    If you're new to IAM, start with AWS-managed policies. These are vetted by AWS and cover common use cases. Over time, you can refine and create customer-managed policies that closely fit your organization's requirements.

Conclusion

IAM policies are your primary toolkit for controlling who gets to do what in AWS. By carefully defining actions, resources, and conditions, you create a precise access control model that safeguards your cloud environment. Remember: start with the principle of least privilege, be explicit in your resources, test your policies, and gradually fine-tune them as your needs evolve.

With a solid understanding of IAM policies, you're now equipped to take a more proactive and security-focused approach to managing identities and permissions in AWS.

Balancing Convenience and Control: AWS-Managed Policies vs. Customer-Managed Policies

When it comes to managing access in AWS, one of the first decisions you'll face is whether to rely on **AWS-managed policies** or create your own **customer-managed policies**. Each approach has its own benefits and trade-offs. Understanding when to use one over the other can help you keep your environment secure, efficient, and aligned with the principle of least privilege.

The Convenience of AWS-Managed Policies

What Are They?
AWS-managed policies are curated sets of permissions maintained and updated by AWS. They're designed to cover common use cases so you don't have to start from scratch each time you need a policy.

Key Advantages:

1. **Easy to Start:**
   Need to quickly provide an administrator full access to your environment or give a new team member read-only privileges to multiple services? AWS-managed policies like AdministratorAccess or ReadOnlyAccess can be attached to a user, group, or role in just a few clicks.
2. **Always Up-to-Date:**
   As AWS services evolve, AWS updates these policies to reflect new features and recommended best practices. This means less overhead for you—no manual edits are required to keep permissions current.
3. **Broad Coverage:**
   You'll find AWS-managed policies for a wide range of scenarios, from full administrative control to role-specific permissions, like AmazonEC2FullAccess or AmazonS3ReadOnlyAccess.

Potential Drawbacks:

- **Over-Permissive by Default:**
  These policies often grant more permissions than you might need. For example, AdministratorAccess opens up the entire AWS environment, which might be too broad for many use cases.

- **No Tweaks Allowed:**
  AWS-managed policies are read-only. If they grant slightly too much access, you can't edit them. Your only option is to create your own custom policy.

The Precision of Customer-Managed Policies

What Are They?
Customer-managed policies are policies you build yourself to fit the exact needs of your organization. Think of them as custom suits tailored to your unique requirements.

Key Advantages:

1. **Full Customization:**
   Need to limit a team's access to a single S3 bucket, allow only certain actions on that bucket, and restrict usage to specific IP ranges? Customer-managed policies give you that level of precision.
2. **Least-Privilege Enforcement:**
   You're in complete control. Instead of relying on pre-set permissions, you define which actions, on which resources, under which conditions are allowed—helping you avoid over-permissioning and adhere to least-privilege principles.
3. **Easier Auditing and Maintenance:**
   Because you name these policies and write them from scratch, they're often easier to understand and audit. Over time, as requirements evolve, you can update them as needed.

Potential Drawbacks:

- **Manual Effort:**
  Creating and maintaining your own policies requires time, expertise, and careful thought. As AWS services grow, you must keep your policies current, which can become a maintenance task in itself.

- **Learning Curve:**
  Crafting a perfectly scoped policy takes practice. You'll
  need to be comfortable with the IAM policy language
  (JSON), actions, resources, and conditions.

When to Use Which?

AWS-Managed Policies:

- **Quick Setup:** If you need to get going fast, say to give a
  test account admin-level access or to provide broad read-
  only visibility, AWS-managed policies are a great start.
- **Standard Use Cases:** If the policy meets your needs as-
  is, why reinvent the wheel? For many standard roles,
  AWS-managed policies might be sufficient.

Customer-Managed Policies:

- **Custom Requirements:** If your organization has strict
  compliance or security requirements—such as granting
  partial access to a single resource—customer-managed
  policies let you be as granular as you need.
- **Security-Critical Roles:** For users or systems that
  handle sensitive operations, tailoring exact permissions
  is worth the effort to ensure no unnecessary access is
  granted.

Real-World Example

Imagine you're onboarding a junior developer who only needs
access to a few non-production S3 buckets to review logs. An
AWS-managed policy like AmazonS3ReadOnlyAccess might
seem suitable at first. But this policy grants read-only access to
all buckets, not just the log buckets. In this case, a customer-
managed policy that allows only s3:GetObject for a specific
bucket (e.g., arn:aws:s3:::company-logs/*) ensures the developer
has the precise level of access needed—no more, no less.

Striking the Right Balance

You're not forced to pick one type of policy and stick with it forever. Many organizations start with AWS-managed policies to get off the ground quickly and gradually replace them with customer-managed policies as they refine their permission strategy. This hybrid approach lets you leverage the convenience of AWS-managed policies in the early stages while steadily adopting stricter, more customized policies as your security maturity grows.

Decision Checklist:

- **Are my requirements straightforward and already covered by an AWS-managed policy?**
  Use AWS-managed.
- **Do I need very specific permissions that no AWS-managed policy provides?**
  Opt for a customer-managed policy.
- **Am I concerned about aligning with least-privilege access from the start?**
  Consider writing a custom policy right away.

Conclusion

AWS-managed policies offer a handy starting point with minimal complexity, while customer-managed policies give you the granularity and customization needed for fine-tuned security. By understanding the strengths and limitations of each, you can choose the right approach—or a blend of both—to maintain a secure and efficient AWS environment.

Enforcing Access Controls with IAM Policies: A Practical Guide

Once you've created the right IAM policies for your organization, the next step is attaching them to the appropriate AWS identities—users, groups, and roles. Assigning policies is at the heart of the principle of least privilege, ensuring each entity gets exactly the permissions it needs—and no more.

In this post, we'll walk through how to attach policies using the AWS Management Console, as well as how to automate assignments with the AWS CLI and API. We'll also cover best practices to help you maintain a secure, scalable access management strategy.

Attaching Policies in the AWS Management Console

For quick, one-off assignments, the AWS Management Console provides an intuitive interface:

1. **Sign In:**
   Log in to the AWS Management Console with administrative credentials.
2. **Open IAM:**
   From the console homepage, go to **IAM**.
3. **Choose Your Identity:**
   o **Users:** Click **Users** in the left sidebar, then pick a user.
   o **Groups:** Click **Groups**, then select the group.
   o **Roles:** Click **Roles**, then pick the role.
4. **Attach a Policy:**
   On the identity's detail page, open the **Permissions** tab and select **Add permissions**. Here, you can:
   o **Attach existing policies directly:** Choose from AWS-managed or customer-managed policies.
   o **Create a policy:** Launch the policy creation wizard if you need something custom.
   o **Copy permissions from existing identities:** Duplicate permissions from another user, group, or role.
5. **Review and Confirm:**
   Double-check your choices and click **Add permissions**.

Example: To give a user read-only access to everything:

- Go to **Users** → **[UserName]** → **Permissions** → **Add permissions**

- Select **Attach existing policies directly** and choose
  ReadOnlyAccess.
- Click **Add permissions**, and you're done!

Automating Policy Assignments with the AWS CLI

For larger-scale operations, the AWS CLI offers a powerful way
to script assignments:

Attach a Managed Policy to a User:

```
aws iam attach-user-policy \
   --user-name JohnDoe \
   --policy-arn arn:aws:iam::aws:policy/ReadOnlyAccess
```

Attach a Managed Policy to a Group:

```
aws iam attach-group-policy \
   --group-name Developers \
   --policy-arn arn:aws:iam::aws:policy/AmazonEC2FullAccess
```

Attach a Managed Policy to a Role:

```
aws iam attach-role-policy \
   --role-name LambdaExecutionRole \
   --policy-arn arn:aws:iam::aws:policy/service-
role/AWSLambdaBasicExecutionRole
```

Inline Policies:
Inline policies are embedded directly into a single user, group, or
role. For example, attaching an inline policy to a user:

```
aws iam put-user-policy \
    --user-name JohnDoe \
    --policy-name S3AccessPolicy \
    --policy-document file://policy.json
```

Attaching Policies Using the AWS API (SDKs)

If you're integrating IAM policy management into your application workflows, SDKs like Python's boto3 let you programmatically manage policies:

Example (Python/boto3):

```
import json
import boto3

iam = boto3.client('iam')

# Attach a managed policy
iam.attach_user_policy(
    UserName='JohnDoe',
    PolicyArn='arn:aws:iam::aws:policy/ReadOnlyAccess'
)

# Attach an inline policy
policy_document = {
  "Version": "2012-10-17",
  "Statement": [
    {
```

```
    "Effect": "Allow",

    "Action": "s3:GetObject",

    "Resource": "arn:aws:s3:::example-bucket/*"

    }

  ]

}


iam.put_user_policy(

  UserName='JohnDoe',

  PolicyName='S3AccessPolicy',

  PolicyDocument=json.dumps(policy_document)

)
```

Best Practices for Assigning Policies

- **Use Groups for Scalability:**
  Instead of attaching policies to individual users, assign
  them to groups. When you add or remove users from the
  group, permissions update automatically.
- **Follow Least Privilege:**
  Grant only the permissions necessary to perform a
  specific job. Avoid using overly broad policies like
  AdministratorAccess for routine tasks.
- **Start with AWS-Managed Policies:**
  For common scenarios (like read-only access), AWS-
  managed policies can save time. As your needs evolve,
  consider customer-managed policies for more granular
  control.
- **Regularly Audit Permissions:**
  Use tools like the IAM Credential Report and Access
  Analyzer to review permissions and identify potential
  security gaps.

- **Combine with Other Security Measures:**
  Policy assignment is just one aspect of a robust security strategy. Pair it with MFA, password policies, and regular access key rotation for comprehensive protection.

Summary

Attaching policies to users, groups, and roles is the final step in ensuring the right people (and services) have the right access at the right time. The AWS Management Console offers a straightforward approach, while the AWS CLI and SDKs provide powerful options for scaling and automating permissions management.

By following best practices—like using groups, avoiding overly permissive policies, and auditing regularly—you'll maintain a secure, organized environment that upholds the principle of least privilege.

Verifying and Fine-Tuning IAM Policies: A Hands-On Guide

It's one thing to write an IAM policy, but ensuring it grants the intended permissions—no more, no less—is another challenge entirely. When users encounter AccessDenied errors or can't perform expected actions, you need to pinpoint where policies are failing. In AWS, you have a powerful ally: the **IAM Policy Simulator**. This built-in tool helps you verify, troubleshoot, and refine your policies before they disrupt critical workflows.

In this post, we'll walk through how to use the Policy Simulator and common strategies for resolving tricky permission issues.

Introducing the IAM Policy Simulator

The IAM Policy Simulator is a web-based tool that lets you test how IAM policies would affect specific requests. Instead of waiting for real-world failures, you can proactively check whether a user, group, or role has the right permissions for the actions they need to perform.

What You Can Do With It:

- **Simulate Actions Across Services:** Check whether your policies allow or deny a given API action, like s3:GetObject or ec2:StartInstances.
- **Evaluate Multiple Policies at Once:** IAM identities often have multiple policies attached. The simulator shows you the combined effect, including any denies that might override allows.
- **Test Resource and Condition Parameters:** Validate that conditions based on IP ranges, specific ARNs, or time constraints work as expected.

How to Use the Policy Simulator

1. **Log In to AWS Management Console:**
   Sign in with credentials that have permissions to view and edit IAM settings.

2. **Open the Policy Simulator:**
   From the **IAM Dashboard**, find the **Policy Simulator** link (or visit the IAM Policy Simulator page directly).
3. **Select the Identity:**
   Choose a user, group, or role you want to test.
4. **Pick an AWS Service and Action:**
   For example, if a user reports they can't download from S3, select **Amazon S3** and the s3:GetObject action.
5. **Specify Conditions (Optional):**
   If your policy uses conditions (like IP-based restrictions), enter these parameters to simulate a realistic scenario.
6. **Run the Simulation:**
   Click **Run Simulation** to see if the action is allowed or denied. If it's denied, the simulator shows you which policy caused the denial.

Example: Troubleshooting S3 Access

Scenario: A user claims they can't download an object from an S3 bucket.

Steps:

- In the Policy Simulator, select the user.
- Choose **S3** as the service and s3:GetObject as the action.
- Specify the bucket ARN (e.g., arn:aws:s3:::example-bucket/*).
- Run the simulation.
- If the result is **Deny**, review the policies attached to see if required actions are missing, if there's an explicit deny, or if resource restrictions are too narrow.

Common Permission Issues and How to Fix Them

1. Missing Permissions
Symptom: You get AccessDenied for a particular action.
Cause: The policy doesn't include the required action.

Fix: Update the policy to include the missing action. For uploading files to S3, add s3:PutObject.

2. Explicit Deny

Symptom: You've allowed an action, but it's still denied.
Cause: An explicit deny overrides any allow.
Fix: Check for Effect: "Deny" in your policies, or Service Control Policies (SCPs) that might be at play. Remove or adjust these deny statements as needed.

3. Resource-Level Restrictions

Symptom: Users can perform actions on some resources but not others.
Cause: The Resource element is too restrictive.
Fix: Make sure the policy's ARNs cover all necessary resources. For S3 objects, use arn:aws:s3:::example-bucket/* to allow actions on all objects in the bucket.

4. Conditions Not Met

Symptom: Permissions fail under certain conditions, like specific IP addresses or time ranges.
Cause: The request doesn't match the conditions in the policy.
Fix: Adjust the condition keys or values. For example, ensure the allowed IP range includes the user's actual IP.

5. Role Trust Policy Issues

Symptom: Users or services can't assume a role even though you've granted permissions.
Cause: The role's trust policy may not include the correct principal.
Fix: Update the trust policy to specify the user, service, or account allowed to assume the role.

6. SCP Restrictions

Symptom: Even though the IAM policy looks correct, actions are still denied.
Cause: An SCP at the organizational level restricts actions.
Fix: Check AWS Organizations for any SCPs. Adjust them to allow the needed actions.

7. Resource-Based Policies

Symptom: Your IAM policies are correct, but access is still denied.

Cause: The resource (like an S3 bucket) has a restrictive resource-based policy.

Fix: Update the resource-based policy to align with the desired access.

Additional Best Practices

- **Leverage CloudTrail Logs:**
  CloudTrail records all API calls in your AWS environment. Reviewing these logs helps you pinpoint where and why access was denied.
- **Use IAM Access Analyzer:**
  IAM Access Analyzer can highlight overly permissive policies or resources shared outside your account, guiding you toward safer configurations.
- **Audit Regularly:**
  Periodic reviews ensure that your policies remain relevant, not overly permissive, and consistent with your evolving security posture.
- **Validate Policy Syntax:**
  Make sure your policies are valid JSON. Even small syntax errors can cause unexpected results.

Bringing It All Together

The IAM Policy Simulator and a systematic approach to diagnosing permission issues are critical for keeping your AWS environment secure and efficient. By proactively testing policies, identifying common pitfalls, and leveraging AWS tools like CloudTrail and Access Analyzer, you can maintain least-privilege access controls and prevent potential downtime or security risks.

With the right processes in place, you'll ensure that your IAM policies do exactly what they're supposed to—nothing more, and nothing less.

Part 2: Advanced IAM Features

Chapter 4: IAM Roles and Temporary Credentials

A Deep Dive into IAM Roles: Elevating Your AWS Security and Flexibility

When building complex architectures in AWS, securing your environment is a top priority. While IAM users provide consistent, long-term access to AWS resources, they might not be the best fit for every scenario—especially when temporary, scoped access is needed. **IAM roles** step in to fill this gap, offering short-lived credentials that can be assumed by people, applications, or services, all without the risk of storing long-term credentials.

In this post, we'll break down what IAM roles are, how they differ from IAM users, and how role chaining and session limits come into play when you're orchestrating multi-account or multi-service workflows.

IAM Roles vs. IAM Users: What's the Difference?

IAM Users:

- Have long-term credentials (passwords, access keys).
- Are tied to a single identity—a person, a tool, or an application—needing persistent access.

IAM Roles:

- Provide **temporary credentials** issued via the AWS Security Token Service (STS).
- Don't have a username, password, or permanent access keys.

- Are "assumed" by an entity (a user, service, or application) that needs temporary access to perform an action.

Key Use Cases for Roles:

1. **Service Access:**
   Allow an AWS service (like EC2 or Lambda) to interact with another service (like S3) on your behalf, without embedding long-term credentials in code.
2. **Cross-Account Access:**
   Grant a user or resource in one AWS account controlled access to specific resources in another, without sharing static credentials.
3. **Federated Access:**
   Integrate external directories or identity providers to give temporary AWS access to corporate users or partners—no permanent credentials required.

In Short: If you need flexible, temporary access without worrying about long-term credential management, IAM roles are your friend.

Role Chaining: A Powerful—but Complex—Feature

Imagine you have a scenario where one role assumes another role, which then assumes another role, and so forth. This is **role chaining**. It's a feature that helps you navigate multi-layered or multi-account environments. The process looks like this:

1. **Initial Assumption:** A user or service assumes a first role.
2. **Subsequent Assumptions:** That role's temporary credentials are used to assume another role, and potentially another, chaining the access through multiple steps.

What's the Benefit?
Role chaining lets you build intricate permission models. For

instance, a developer in a central AWS account can assume a "primary role" that, in turn, gives them the ability to assume a "secondary role" in another AWS account, granting access to resources there—without ever hard-coding credentials.

But Beware of Complexity:
While technically there's no hard upper limit on chaining roles, more links in the chain mean more complexity. Too many chained roles can become confusing to manage, audit, and secure.

Understanding Session Limits

Session Duration:
The temporary credentials you get from assuming a role don't last forever. You choose a session duration (from 15 minutes up to 12 hours for most roles). Shorter sessions reduce exposure but might inconvenience workflows that need longer uninterrupted access.

Depth of Chaining:
While not hard-limited by AWS, an extensive role chain can complicate troubleshooting and increase the risk of misconfigurations. Aim for simplicity—fewer roles, cleaner workflows.

Credential Expiration:
Each new set of temporary credentials issued by STS inherits its own expiration time. Once the last role in the chain issues temporary credentials, that's the timer you're on. When they expire, you'll need to re-initiate the role assumption process.

Best Practices for Managing Roles and Role Chaining

1. **Keep Chains Short:**
   Minimize how many roles you chain together. The simpler the path, the easier it is to maintain security, understand permissions, and troubleshoot issues.

49

2. **Monitor Assumptions:**
   Use AWS CloudTrail to log all role assumptions. Keeping an eye on these logs helps you detect unusual patterns or potential security incidents.
3. **Right-Size Session Durations:**
   For sensitive operations, shorter durations limit the time compromised credentials could be used. For routine tasks, find a duration that balances security with convenience.
4. **Leverage Conditions:**
   Use IAM policy conditions to control which identities can assume a role. For example, you can restrict a particular role to only be assumed by a specific "primary role," effectively limiting who can chain roles together.

Example Condition:

json

Copy code

```
{
  "Effect": "Allow",
  "Action": "sts:AssumeRole",
  "Resource": "arn:aws:iam::123456789012:role/ChainedRole",
  "Condition": {
    "StringEquals": {
      "aws:CalledVia":
"arn:aws:iam::123456789012:role/PrimaryRole"
    }
  }
}
```

This ensures only the PrimaryRole can assume ChainedRole, preventing unauthorized chaining.

Bringing It All Together

IAM roles are a cornerstone of secure, flexible access management in AWS. By eliminating the need for long-term credentials, roles reduce your risk footprint. They're essential when giving AWS services or external identities controlled access to resources.

Role chaining provides an elegant way to navigate complex, multi-account setups—but should be used sparingly and managed with care. Always keep a close eye on session durations, credential expiration, and the complexity of your role chain. By following best practices—short chains, frequent monitoring, careful session duration choices, and restrictive conditions—you'll ensure that your IAM roles and role chains work for you, not against you.

In essence: Use roles to empower agile, secure, and versatile access. Keep your chains short, your durations right-sized, and your conditions tight—and you'll reap the full benefits of IAM roles in your AWS environment.

Chapter 5: Advanced Policy Management

Mastering Complex IAM Policies: A Deep Dive into JSON-Based Permissions

As your AWS infrastructure grows, so does the complexity of managing access to its resources. **AWS Identity and Access Management (IAM)** policies are the backbone of your security strategy, giving you precise control over who can do what—and under what conditions. But crafting complex IAM policies can seem daunting at first. Understanding the key elements, leveraging wildcards, and using variables can help you write powerful, flexible, and secure JSON policies that scale with your environment.

Core Policy Elements: Principal, Effect, and Action

Every IAM policy consists of a few essential components. Get these right, and you'll have a strong foundation for building out more complex rules.

1. Principal:
The **Principal** element defines *who* the policy applies to. This can be an IAM user, role, AWS account, AWS service, or a federated identity. By specifying principals, you effectively say, "These permissions apply to this specific identity."

Examples:

```
"Principal": {

  "AWS": "arn:aws:iam::123456789012:role/ExampleRole"

}
```

```
"Principal": {

  "Service": "lambda.amazonaws.com"

}
```

2. Effect:
The **Effect** element states whether you're allowing or denying a requested action. Explicit denies override all allows, so be careful when you use them.

Example:

```
"Effect": "Allow"
```

3. Action:
The **Action** element specifies the AWS API operations covered

by the policy. You can grant or deny granular actions (like s3:PutObject) or use wildcards to cover multiple actions at once ("s3:Get*" to allow all S3 "Get" actions).

Examples:

"Action": "s3:ListBucket"

"Action": "ec2:StartInstances"

Harnessing the Power of Wildcards and Variables

To write truly dynamic, flexible policies, you'll need to go beyond static ARNs and actions.

Wildcards (*):
Wildcards let you match multiple resources, actions, or conditions without enumerating each one. For example, s3:Get* covers all S3 "Get" actions, and arn:aws:s3:::example-bucket/* covers every object in a given bucket.

Variables (${}):
Variables inject context into your policy. For instance, ${aws:username} references the current user's name, enabling user-specific controls without writing separate policies for each identity.

Examples:

"Resource": "arn:aws:s3:::example-bucket/${aws:username}/*"

This line grants each user access only to their own folder inside example-bucket.

Combining Conditions for Fine-Grained Control

Complex policies often involve conditions—key-value pairs that specify when a policy statement applies. Conditions can restrict actions by IP address, region, date and time, presence of MFA, and more. Together with wildcards and variables, conditions help you create highly customized rules.

Example Condition:

```
"Condition": {
 "IpAddress": {
  "aws:SourceIp": "203.0.113.0/24"
 },
 "StringEquals": {
  "aws:region": "us-east-1"
 }
}
```

This ensures the allowed action is only valid if requests originate from a specific IP range and occur in us-east-1.

A Real-World Example: Complex S3 Policy

Scenario: Suppose you want to let IAM users upload files to S3, but only into folders named after their usernames, only if they connect from a certain IP range, and only in a specific region.

Policy:

```
{
  "Version": "2012-10-17",
  "Statement": [
    {
      "Effect": "Allow",
      "Action": "s3:PutObject",
      "Resource": "arn:aws:s3:::example-bucket/${aws:username}/*",
      "Condition": {
        "IpAddress": {
          "aws:SourceIp": "203.0.113.0/24"
        },
        "StringEquals": {
          "aws:region": "us-east-1"
        }
      }
    }
  ]
}
```

What's happening here?

- **Customized Resources:** ${aws:username} ensures each user's access is restricted to their own directory.
- **Network Restrictions:** IpAddress condition keys limit access by IP, adding a network-based security layer.
- **Geographic/Regional Constraints:** StringEquals on aws:region ensures actions only occur in us-east-1.

Best Practices for Writing Complex IAM Policies

1. **Principle of Least Privilege:**
   Give the minimum necessary permissions. Avoid * on everything unless absolutely needed.
2. **Use AWS-Managed Policies for Common Cases:**
   If there's a straightforward scenario, start with AWS-managed policies and customize them as needed.
3. **Test Before Deploying:**
   The **IAM Policy Simulator** is your friend. Test policies to ensure they behave as intended before putting them into production.
4. **Document Complex Policies:**
   Add comments in your code repository or maintain external documentation. Complex policies can be difficult to understand at a glance.
5. **Regularly Review and Update:**
   Infrastructure and organizational needs change over time. Regular audits help maintain least privilege and adapt to new requirements.

Summing Up

Crafting complex IAM policies might seem challenging, but it's a powerful tool for securing your AWS environment. By mastering the use of principals, effects, actions, wildcards, variables, and conditions, you can write policies that are both flexible and fine-grained. With careful testing and adherence to best practices, you'll create policies that perfectly align with your organization's evolving security and governance needs.

Enhancing IAM Security with Conditional Policies

IAM policies don't have to be static; by incorporating conditions, you can make your permissions dynamic, context-aware, and more secure. Conditions let you refine access control rules based on factors like the requester's IP address, the current time, the AWS region, or whether MFA is in use. This extra layer of granularity helps ensure that only the right people, from the right places, at the right times, have access to your AWS resources.

Introducing Conditions in IAM Policies

Conditions in IAM policies use **condition keys**—predefined attributes provided by AWS or specific services—that can be matched against values you define. With these keys and the appropriate condition operators, you can fine-tune permissions far beyond simple "allow" and "deny" statements.

Common Condition Keys Include:

- aws:SourceIp: Restrict access by IP address or CIDR range.
- aws:CurrentTime: Limit actions to certain time windows.
- aws:MultiFactorAuthPresent: Ensure MFA is used for sensitive operations.
- aws:SecureTransport: Require HTTPS to guarantee secure connections.

Service-specific keys (like those for S3 or EC2) let you tailor conditions even more closely to each service's unique capabilities and resource types.

Practical Examples

IP-Based Restrictions:
Limit S3 bucket access to a specific IP range:

```
"Condition": {
  "IpAddress": { "aws:SourceIp": "203.0.113.0/24" }
}
```

1.

Time-Based Access:
Allow EC2 instance starting only during business hours:

```
"Condition": {
  "DateGreaterThan": { "aws:CurrentTime": "2023-12-07T09:00:00Z" },
  "DateLessThan": { "aws:CurrentTime": "2023-12-07T17:00:00Z" }
}
```

2.

Secure Connections Only:
Deny all actions if not using HTTPS:

```
"Condition": {
  "Bool": { "aws:SecureTransport": "false" }
}
```

3.

MFA Enforcement:
Require MFA for S3 bucket access:

```
"Condition": {
  "Bool": { "aws:MultiFactorAuthPresent": "true" }
}
```

4.

Region Restriction:
Allow RDS actions only in us-east-1:

```
"Condition": {
  "StringEquals": { "aws:RequestedRegion": "us-east-1" }
}
```

5.

Best Practices for Conditional Policies

- **Combine Multiple Conditions:**
  String together conditions (e.g., IP and time) for even tighter controls.
- **Test Before Applying:**
  Use the **IAM Policy Simulator** to ensure your conditions work as intended.
- **Maintain Least Privilege:**
  Conditions help enforce the principle of least privilege by granting access only in precisely defined scenarios.
- **Regular Reviews:**
  Update conditions periodically to keep up with changing IP ranges, business hours, or compliance requirements.

Takeaway

By leveraging conditions in IAM policies, you move from simple "who can do what" permissions to a more nuanced "who can do what, when, where, and under what circumstances." This transforms your security model into one that's both adaptive and tightly controlled, ultimately strengthening the overall resilience and integrity of your AWS environment.

Introducing Attribute-Based Access Control (ABAC): Dynamic, Flexible, and Scalable

As organizations scale their AWS environments, traditional Role-Based Access Control (RBAC) models can quickly become unwieldy. Enter **Attribute-Based Access Control (ABAC)**—a permissions model that relies on resource tags and identity attributes rather than fixed roles. By evaluating context-sensitive conditions, ABAC enables dynamic, flexible, and scalable access management that adapts seamlessly to changing requirements and large infrastructures.

What is ABAC?

Attribute-Based Access Control (ABAC) uses attributes—key-value pairs attached to AWS resources, users, or roles—to determine who has access. Rather than assigning permissions to roles and then mapping users to those roles, ABAC policies look for matching tags. If the tags on a resource align with the tags on the requesting identity, access is granted.

Example:

- A user or role might have the tag Project: Development.
- An EC2 instance could be tagged Project: Development.
- An ABAC policy allows actions only if aws:PrincipalTag/Project equals aws:ResourceTag/Project.
- Result: The user automatically gains access to the correct instances without administrators modifying roles or policies each time a new instance appears.

How ABAC Works

1. **Tag Your Resources:**
   Assign tags to AWS resources that reflect their characteristics—such as Environment: Production or Team: Engineering.

2. **Tag Your Identities:**
   Tag IAM users or roles with attributes that describe their responsibilities or affiliations, like Project: Development.
3. **Create an ABAC Policy:**
   Use condition keys in your IAM policy to compare the principal's tags (aws:PrincipalTag) with resource tags (aws:ResourceTag).

Example Policy:

```
{
  "Version": "2012-10-17",
  "Statement": [
    {
      "Effect": "Allow",
      "Action": "s3:*",
      "Resource": "arn:aws:s3:::*",
      "Condition": {
        "StringEquals": {
          "aws:ResourceTag/Project": "${aws:PrincipalTag/Project}"
        }
      }
    }
  ]
}
```

Here, users gain access to only those S3 buckets whose Project tag matches their own Project attribute.

61

Advanced ABAC Use Cases

- **Restricting EC2 Actions by Team:**
  Allow starting or stopping EC2 instances only if the user's Team tag matches the instance's Team tag.
- **Enforcing Required Tags on Creation:**
  Deny the creation of new instances unless the user includes a specific tag like Environment: Production.

Why Choose ABAC Over RBAC?

1. **Scalability:**
   - **ABAC:** Grows effortlessly with your environment. As new resources and users appear, consistent tagging ensures policies automatically adapt.
   - **RBAC:** Requires continuous role creation and reassignment, leading to complexity and overhead as the environment expands.
2. **Flexibility:**
   - **ABAC:** Modify access instantly by adding or changing tags. If a developer moves to a different project, just update their tags—no need to recreate or map roles.
   - **RBAC:** Adjusting roles and group memberships often involves manual work and policy reconfigurations.
3. **Simplified Policy Management:**
   - **ABAC:** One policy can cover numerous scenarios, thanks to tag-based conditions.
   - **RBAC:** Frequently spawns a complex web of roles and policies, making governance harder.
4. **Improved Security:**
   - **ABAC:** Enforces least privilege at scale. If a resource isn't tagged to match a user's attributes, that user can't access it.
   - **RBAC:** Static roles may grant broader permissions than necessary.
5. **Automation-Friendly:**

- ○ **ABAC:** Perfect for ephemeral or dynamic environments (like CI/CD pipelines and auto-scaling). Newly created resources inherit tags automatically, and access adjusts without manual intervention.
- ○ **RBAC:** Less agile, as predefined roles may not align well with on-the-fly resource changes.

Best Practices for ABAC

1. **Consistent Tagging Conventions:**
   Define a standard set of tags (e.g., Project, Team, Environment) and ensure every new resource and identity follows these rules.
2. **Combine ABAC with RBAC:** Use ABAC for large-scale, dynamic resource sets and RBAC for more static, organizational-level roles. This hybrid approach lets you enjoy the best of both worlds.
3. **Test and Validate Policies:** Use the **IAM Policy Simulator** to confirm that your tag-based conditions work as intended before deploying them into production.
4. **Regularly Audit Tags:** Ensure tags are maintained accurately over time. Use AWS Config or tagging enforcement policies to detect untagged or improperly tagged resources.

Conclusion

ABAC offers a powerful alternative to traditional RBAC by leveraging tags to grant permissions dynamically. It simplifies policy management, adapts quickly to organizational changes, and strengthens your security posture. In today's fast-paced, cloud-driven environments, ABAC can be the key to effective, scalable, and secure identity and access management.

Elevating Your IAM Game: Validating Policies with AWS Tools

In the world of AWS Identity and Access Management (IAM), creating well-structured policies is only half the battle. Ensuring they work as intended—without granting unnecessary privileges or causing accidental lockouts—can be tricky, especially as your cloud environment becomes more complex. That's where policy validation tools come into play.

AWS provides two powerful resources to help you audit and refine your IAM policies:

1. **IAM Policy Simulator**: Ideal for testing and troubleshooting the effects of IAM policies on hypothetical requests.
2. **IAM Access Analyzer**: Designed to highlight overly permissive or risky configurations, enabling you to tighten security postures before they become a problem.

By weaving these tools into your policy management workflow, you can confidently deliver secure, least-privilege access to your users and services.

IAM Policy Simulator: Try Before You Apply

Before rolling out a new policy—or updating an existing one—wouldn't it be nice to know exactly how it behaves? The **IAM Policy Simulator** lets you do just that. Think of it as a sandbox where you can try out API calls and see if your policies would grant or deny the requested actions.

How It Works:

1. **Select the Identity**: Choose a user, group, or role, or just paste in a policy's JSON definition.

2. **Pick the Actions and Services**: From listing S3 buckets to starting EC2 instances, simulate whatever action you want to validate.
3. **Run the Simulation**: The tool shows whether the call would be allowed or denied. If denied, you'll see which policy or condition caused the block.

When to Use It:

- **Debugging Permissions**: A user can't delete an S3 object they should have access to? Simulate s3:DeleteObject and find out which policy is holding them back.
- **Previewing Changes**: Introducing a new policy or adding conditions? Simulate API calls first to ensure you're not inadvertently locking down access or leaving a backdoor open.

Pro Tip:

Simulate realistic scenarios by specifying resource ARNs and conditions—like IP addresses or request times—to ensure your policies behave correctly under production-like conditions.

IAM Access Analyzer: Spotting Risks Before They Emerge

While the Policy Simulator focuses on operational correctness, **IAM Access Analyzer** takes a more strategic view. Its job is to continuously scan your environment's resource policies (like those on S3 buckets, KMS keys, or IAM roles) and point out configurations that might allow unintended external or public access.

Key Capabilities:

- **Public Access Alerts**: Identify if anyone on the internet can access your S3 bucket.
- **Cross-Account Sharing**: See if a sensitive resource is accessible from another AWS account that shouldn't have that privilege.
- **Actionable Recommendations**: For each finding, Access Analyzer suggests changes to tighten resource policies.

When to Use It:

- **Security Audits**: Periodically check to ensure no resource has drifted into being publicly accessible or incorrectly shared.
- **Compliance and Governance**: Show auditors that you have a continuous, automated tool assessing your policies for misconfigurations.

Pro Tip:

After addressing a flagged issue, re-run Access Analyzer to confirm that your changes fixed the problem. This iterative approach helps maintain a clean security posture over time.

Using Both Tools in Harmony

IAM Policy Simulator is like a magnifying glass, helping you inspect detailed policy interactions for specific actions. **IAM Access Analyzer** is more like a spotlight, shining across your entire account to reveal broader risks.

By combining both:

1. **Fine-Tune Individual Policies with the Simulator**: Ensure each policy grants only the necessary permissions.
2. **Audit Overall Security with Access Analyzer**: Continuously monitor for policies that might expose resources to unintended parties.

Example Scenario:

- **Step 1 (Simulator)**: You've created a policy to let developers read from a particular S3 bucket but not write to it. Run the Policy Simulator to confirm that s3:GetObject is allowed and s3:PutObject is denied.
- **Step 2 (Access Analyzer)**: Down the line, Access Analyzer flags that the same S3 bucket is publicly accessible due to a bucket policy. Armed with this insight, you revisit the bucket policy and remove the offending statements—then run Access Analyzer again to confirm the fix.

Best Practices for Policy Validation

1. **Integrate Early and Often**: Don't wait for a security incident to start using these tools. Incorporate policy validation into your development and deployment cycles.
2. **Automate in CI/CD**: Use the Policy Simulator and Access Analyzer as part of your CI/CD pipeline. Automatically test policies before they ever hit production.
3. **Document and Audit Regularly**: Maintain a record of identified issues and resolutions. Regular audits ensure policies remain aligned with evolving best practices and compliance requirements.

4. **Combine with Other Security Measures**: Use IAM Access Analyzer findings along with AWS Config rules, GuardDuty alerts, or Security Hub insights to build a comprehensive security posture.

Wrapping Up

IAM policies are the guardrails of your AWS environment, controlling who can do what, where, and when. But without validation, you're operating in the dark—hoping your policies behave as intended. The IAM Policy Simulator and IAM Access Analyzer shine a light on your policies, helping you catch misconfigurations, tighten permissions, and keep your environment secure.

By integrating these tools into your workflows, you'll move from guesswork to certainty, ensuring that every IAM policy aligns perfectly with your organization's security and compliance objectives.

Part 3: Expert IAM Practices

Chapter 6: Enhancing IAM Security

Strengthening Your AWS Security Posture with MFA Enforcement

In today's security landscape, relying on a single factor of authentication—like a password—is no longer sufficient to keep threats at bay. **Multi-Factor Authentication (MFA)** adds another layer of protection, significantly reducing the risk of unauthorized access, even if a user's credentials are compromised. By enforcing MFA in AWS, you ensure that attackers can't simply log in and pivot throughout your environment with stolen passwords. Instead, users must prove their identity through an additional factor, such as a one-time code from a virtual device or a hardware security key.

In this post, we'll explore how to set up MFA for your IAM users, implement conditional policies to enforce MFA for sensitive actions, and maintain ongoing visibility into MFA compliance across your AWS accounts.

Setting Up MFA for IAM Users

Getting started with MFA is straightforward:

1. **Sign In with Admin Credentials:**
   Log in to the AWS Management Console as the root user or an admin-level IAM user.
2. **Head to the IAM Dashboard:**
   From the console, open **IAM → Users**, and select the IAM user you want to protect with MFA.
3. **Manage MFA Devices:**
   On the user's detail page, select **Security Credentials → Manage MFA Device**. You can choose from:

- ○ **Virtual MFA Devices:** Use apps like Google Authenticator or Authy.
- ○ **Hardware MFA Devices:** Physical tokens (e.g., YubiKey) for high-security scenarios.
4. **Follow Setup Prompts:**
  For virtual MFA, scan the QR code with your app and enter the two one-time codes displayed. For hardware devices, provide the serial number and two consecutive OTPs.
5. **Verify and Complete Setup:**
  Once verified, MFA is active, and the user must provide a one-time code at each login.

Best Practices:

- • **Enable MFA on the Root Account Immediately:** The root user has unrestricted access—securing it should be your top priority.
- • **Use Virtual MFA for Portability:** Virtual tokens on smartphones are easy and convenient.
- • **Consider Hardware MFA for Admins:** Hardware keys provide an added layer of assurance for highly privileged accounts.

Enforcing MFA with Conditional Policies

Enabling MFA is great, but it doesn't guarantee that users will always use it. Conditional policies let you enforce MFA as a requirement for performing certain actions or accessing specific resources.

How It Works:

- • Use the aws:MultiFactorAuthPresent condition key in your IAM policies.
- • If aws:MultiFactorAuthPresent is false, deny access to critical actions or resources.

Example: Require MFA for S3:

```
{
  "Version": "2012-10-17",
  "Statement": [
    {
      "Effect": "Deny",
      "Action": "s3:*",
      "Resource": "*",
      "Condition": {
      "BoolIfExists": {
        "aws:MultiFactorAuthPresent": "false"
      }
    }
  }
  ]
}
```

Explanation: This policy denies all S3 actions unless the user has authenticated with MFA. Users who skip MFA won't be able to interact with any S3 buckets or objects.

You can tweak this approach further to only require MFA for sensitive actions—like deleting resources—or apply it across your entire AWS environment for an ironclad security stance.

71

Monitoring and Auditing MFA Compliance

Once MFA is enforced, you need to ensure that users are consistently adhering to it. Regular checks help maintain compliance and catch any drifting configurations.

Key Tools for Ongoing Visibility:

1. **IAM Credential Reports:**
   From the IAM Dashboard, generate a Credential Report. It shows which users have MFA enabled (MFA Active column). Download this CSV periodically to confirm compliance.
2. **AWS Config Rules:**
   Enable AWS Config and use the iam-user-mfa-enabled managed rule. It continuously checks all IAM users and flags those who don't have MFA activated.
3. **AWS CloudTrail Logs:**
   Monitor CloudTrail for actions taken without MFA. Although your policies should block such actions, CloudTrail logs can reveal attempts or misconfigurations.

Why Enforce MFA?

1. Enhanced Security:
MFA requires something you know (password) plus something you have (OTP device or hardware key). Attackers who only have the password still can't break in.

2. Regulatory Compliance:
MFA aligns with many industry standards and compliance frameworks like PCI DSS, ISO 27001, and SOC 2, often simplifying your audit process.

3. Flexible and Granular Control:
Conditional policies let you apply MFA requirements

selectively. Tailor MFA to your organization's workflow—maybe all developers must use MFA for production actions, while read-only access remains more relaxed.

Best Practices for MFA Enforcement

- **Mandate MFA for Privileged Accounts:** Ensure that admins and power users face stricter controls.
- **Educate and Onboard Users:** Provide clear instructions and training. If MFA feels cumbersome, users might resist.
- **Combine MFA with Other Controls:** Use MFA alongside well-designed IAM policies, tag-based (ABAC) controls, and least-privilege principles for a holistic security strategy.
- **Automate Checks and Notifications:** Integrate MFA checks into CI/CD pipelines, use AWS Config for continuous compliance, and set up alerts for any user missing MFA.

Final Thoughts

MFA is a fundamental security practice, raising the bar significantly for attackers. By setting up MFA for IAM users, using conditional policies to enforce it for sensitive actions, and continuously auditing compliance, you ensure that your AWS environment remains resilient against credential theft and unauthorized access.

Making MFA mandatory might feel like an extra step for your team initially, but the peace of mind and heightened security far outweigh the inconvenience. In a world where threats evolve rapidly, MFA stands as a simple yet powerful defense against unauthorized access to your AWS resources.

Building a Lean, Secure AWS Environment: Least-Privilege Access Best Practices

In an era of increasing cybersecurity threats and compliance demands, the principle of **least-privilege access** stands as a cornerstone of secure and efficient AWS operations. By ensuring that each identity—be it a user, group, or role—has only the exact permissions required to do their job, you significantly reduce the attack surface and curb the potential fallout of compromised credentials or insider threats.

In this post, we'll explore how to maintain a least-privilege environment through regular permission reviews and the use of IAM Access Analyzer, giving you a comprehensive strategy to keep your AWS environment both agile and safe.

Start with Regular Permission Reviews

When was the last time you checked if every user in your AWS account truly needs the permissions they currently have? Permissions often stack up over time as teams experiment with new services or as roles evolve, leaving behind unnecessary and sometimes risky access. A consistent review process helps nip these issues in the bud.

How to Review Permissions:

1. **Generate an IAM Credential Report:**
   In the IAM Dashboard, generate a credential report. This CSV file shows which users have active credentials, when they last logged in, and whether MFA is enabled. It's an excellent starting point to spot dormant accounts or unused access keys.
2. **Check Access with "Last Accessed" Data:**
   AWS IAM provides "last accessed" information for services and actions within policies. By reviewing how

recently a permission was used, you can safely remove policies for idle services without breaking workflows.

3. **Audit and Update Policies:**
    o Identify overly broad policies that use wildcards (*), and replace them with more granular, resource-specific permissions.
    o Remove policies that haven't been used in months.
    o Rotate access keys regularly and remove keys that are no longer needed.
4. **Use CloudTrail and AWS Config:**
    o **CloudTrail**: Examine API call history to confirm which permissions are truly required.
    o **AWS Config**: Apply rules (like iam-user-no-policies) to identify and prevent policy misconfigurations.

Example Workflow:

* Download the IAM Credential Report and look for inactive users or unused keys.
* Use IAM's "Access Advisor" on policies to see which services haven't been touched recently.
* Remove or tighten permissions accordingly.

Leverage IAM Access Analyzer for Continuous Validation

While manual audits are important, they can be time-consuming. That's where **IAM Access Analyzer** steps in—automating the identification of overly permissive or risky resource policies. It continuously scans your environment, highlighting which buckets, roles, or keys are accessible by external accounts or the general public.

Key Features of IAM Access Analyzer:

- **Detect Public and Cross-Account Access:** Identify resources—like S3 buckets—open to the internet or shared too broadly.
- **Actionable Findings:** Each finding comes with clear recommendations for how to limit access.
- **Policy Validation:** Check new policies before deployment to ensure they conform to least-privilege principles.

How to Use It:

1. **Create an Analyzer:**
   Within the IAM dashboard, set up an analyzer to monitor your resources (e.g., S3 buckets, IAM roles).
2. **Review Findings:**
   Receive alerts about any resource that grants undue access. A common example is an S3 bucket with a Principal: "*" statement, making it publicly accessible.
3. **Remediate and Validate:**
   Update the resource's policy to restrict access (perhaps to a specific IAM role or account) and rerun the analyzer to confirm the fix.

Example Use Case:

- Access Analyzer flags an S3 bucket as publicly readable.
- You remove the public access statement from its policy.
- Re-run the analyzer to ensure no external account can now access the bucket.

Best Practices for a Robust Least-Privilege Model

1. **Enable Continuous Monitoring:**
   Set up IAM Access Analyzer to run continuously so that

any new resource or policy introduced into your environment is immediately evaluated.

2. **Validate Policy Changes Early:**
   Before applying a new policy, use the "Validate Policy" feature in Access Analyzer. Catching issues early reduces the risk of inadvertently creating security gaps.

3. **Automate Remediation:**
   Pair Access Analyzer with AWS Lambda functions to automatically remediate certain types of risky access. For example, if a bucket becomes public, a Lambda function can restrict it automatically.

4. **Combine Tools for Comprehensive Security:**
   Use Access Analyzer in tandem with Config rules and Security Hub. This integrated approach ensures you have visibility and automated checks across multiple layers of your AWS environment.

Why All This Matters

Proactive Risk Mitigation:
By regularly reviewing permissions and using Access Analyzer, you spot and address vulnerabilities before attackers can exploit them.

Improved Compliance:
Many regulatory standards require strong access controls. Demonstrating a robust least-privilege model helps meet PCI DSS, ISO 27001, and other compliance mandates.

Efficient Policy Management:
A well-managed least-privilege strategy prevents "policy sprawl," where hundreds of overlapping, broad policies make your environment unwieldy and error-prone.

Stronger Security Posture:
By ensuring every permission serves a purpose and no resource

is overexposed, you build a lean, resilient, and trustworthy AWS environment.

Bringing It All Together

Least-privilege access isn't a one-and-done configuration—it's an ongoing process of refinement, validation, and vigilance. Regular permission audits ensure that identities aren't clinging to unnecessary powers. IAM Access Analyzer provides a continuous check, raising the alarm whenever a policy drifts toward dangerous over-permissiveness.

By adopting these best practices, you ensure that every door in your AWS environment is only as open as it needs to be, reducing risk, improving compliance, and maintaining a strong, secure foundation for your operations in the cloud.

Chapter 7: IAM for Multi-Account Environments

Bringing Order to the Chaos: Managing IAM in Multi-Account AWS Setups

As your AWS footprint grows, relying on a single account to house all your workloads quickly becomes cumbersome and risky. Adopting a multi-account strategy—separating environments for development, testing, and production, or grouping accounts by team or project—helps isolate risks, improve governance, and streamline billing.

However, managing Identity and Access Management (IAM) in a multi-account environment isn't just about more accounts. It's about ensuring that each account adheres to enterprise-wide security standards, while still giving individual teams the autonomy to innovate. In this post, we'll explore how AWS Organizations, Service Control Policies (SCPs), and other cross-account access strategies can help you achieve centralized governance, robust security, and seamless collaboration.

Introducing AWS Organizations and SCPs

AWS Organizations is your command center for overseeing multiple AWS accounts. It provides a hierarchical structure that lets you group accounts into Organizational Units (OUs) aligned with departments, projects, or environments, all under a single management umbrella. With consolidated billing and centralized governance, you gain transparency and control at scale.

Service Control Policies (SCPs) extend your governance capabilities by acting as high-level guardrails. While IAM policies grant permissions to users and roles, SCPs define the *maximum* permissions that member accounts can have. They don't grant access themselves, but they ensure no account—no matter how lax a local admin tries to be—can ever exceed your established security baseline.

Example: You can apply an SCP to your "Development" OU that denies S3 bucket creation. This prevents developers from creating new buckets arbitrarily, maintaining order and protecting your environment.

Getting Started with AWS Organizations and SCPs

1. **Create an Organization:**
    Log in as the management account and set up AWS Organizations. Add existing accounts or create new ones under your organizational umbrella.
2. **Organize Accounts into OUs:**
    Group accounts based on environment or function—like "Development" and "Production" OUs. This logical structure lets you apply different controls to different parts of your enterprise.
3. **Write and Attach SCPs:**
    SCPs are JSON-based policies similar to IAM policies, but at the organizational level. Attach them to your root, OU, or individual accounts. For example, an SCP might prohibit disabling CloudTrail logging or restrict actions to certain regions.
4. **Monitor and Adjust:**
    Use CloudTrail logs and other monitoring tools to ensure that your SCPs are working as intended. Adjust them over time as your needs evolve.

Benefits of SCPs:

-   Centralized control over what's allowed and what's off-limits.
-   The assurance that no account can bypass these foundational rules.
-   A consistent, secure baseline across your entire AWS footprint.

Enabling Cross-Account Resource Sharing

In a multi-account setup, it's common for workloads in one account to need access to resources in another. AWS offers several methods to securely enable cross-account access, each suited to different scenarios:

1. IAM Roles for Cross-Account Access:
Create a role in the target account that grants the necessary permissions, and allow the source account's users or roles to assume it. This approach keeps long-term credentials out of the picture and provides a clear audit trail of who accessed what and when.

2. Resource-Based Policies:
Attach a policy directly to a resource—like an S3 bucket or a KMS key—to allow another account's identities to access it. This method is straightforward for read-only scenarios or simple sharing rules.

3. AWS Resource Access Manager (RAM):
Use AWS RAM to share resources like VPC subnets, Transit Gateways, or Aurora DB clusters without fiddling with IAM policies. Just create a resource share, invite specific accounts, and manage it all centrally.

4. Organizations Service Access:
For even broader stroke policies, integrate your resource sharing with AWS Organizations. By referencing the organization's ID in a resource policy, you can grant access to every account in the organization, ensuring seamless scale without repetitive per-account configurations.

Best Practices for Multi-Account IAM

1. **Use SCPs as a Safety Net:**
   Start by applying restrictive SCPs at the root or OU

81

level—like denying any action that disables logging or encryption. Adjust these SCPs as you trust and refine your environment.

2. **Keep Cross-Account Permissions Minimal:**
   Follow the principle of least privilege across accounts. Give just enough access to fulfill a use case and regularly review these configurations.

3. **Audit and Monitor Activity:**
   CloudTrail and AWS Config are your allies. Continuously monitor account activities and resource configurations to ensure compliance with your security policies.

4. **Enable Centralized Logging:**
   Collect logs (like CloudTrail, Config, and CloudWatch logs) in a central "logging" or "security" account, making it easier to detect anomalies and enforce standards.

5. **Leverage Tags and Metadata:**
   Tag accounts and resources to keep track of who owns what and why. Tags help you navigate the complexity of multi-account environments and apply policies programmatically.

Bringing It All Together

Multi-account setups offer the flexibility and compartmentalization modern organizations need, but they also introduce complexity. By using AWS Organizations and SCPs as your governance backbone, and by employing smart cross-account access strategies, you can maintain tight security and compliance without sacrificing autonomy and innovation.

A robust multi-account strategy ensures that as your AWS usage grows, your security and compliance posture scales with it. With careful planning, continuous auditing, and a well-structured approach to IAM, you'll create an environment where every account, resource, and identity plays nicely together—under the watchful eye of your centralized governance framework.

Chapter 8: IAM and Federated Identity Management

Federation Protocols in AWS: SAML and OpenID Connect

AWS Identity and Access Management (IAM) supports federation protocols like **SAML (Security Assertion Markup Language)** and **OpenID Connect (OIDC)** to streamline access for users authenticated through external identity providers (IdPs). By leveraging these protocols, organizations can integrate AWS with corporate directories or third-party IdPs, eliminating the need to create IAM users for every individual.

SAML-Based Federation

SAML enables secure integration between external IdPs (e.g., Okta, Azure AD) and AWS. Users authenticated by the IdP can assume AWS IAM roles for resource access, simplifying user management and enhancing security.

Steps to Set Up SAML Federation

1. **Configure the Identity Provider in AWS**
   - Log in to the AWS Management Console.
   - Navigate to **IAM → Identity Providers**.
   - Click **Add Provider**, select **SAML**, and upload the IdP's metadata XML file.
2. **Create an IAM Role for Federation**
   - Go to **IAM → Roles → Create Role**.
   - Select **SAML 2.0 Federation** and choose the SAML provider.
   - Attach policies to define role permissions (e.g., ReadOnlyAccess).
3. **Configure the IdP**
   - In the IdP, create an application for AWS.

84

- o Enter the AWS account ID, role ARN, and SAML assertion consumer URL (https://signin.aws.amazon.com/saml).
4. **Test the Federation**
   - o Log in to the IdP and access the AWS application.
   - o Verify successful redirection to AWS with the assumed role.

SAML Assertion Example

A SAML assertion for AWS typically includes attributes mapping users to IAM roles:

```
<saml2:AttributeStatement>
  <saml2:Attribute
Name="https://aws.amazon.com/SAML/Attributes/Role">
    <saml2:AttributeValue>
      arn:aws:iam::123456789012:role/ExampleRole,arn:aws:iam::123456789012:saml-provider/ExampleProvider
    </saml2:AttributeValue>
  </saml2:Attribute>
</saml2:AttributeStatement>
```

Best Practices for SAML Federation

- **Use Session Tags:** Include user attributes in SAML assertions for dynamic access control.
- **Enforce MFA:** Require multi-factor authentication at the IdP level.
- **Monitor Activity:** Use CloudTrail to log federated role assumptions.

Using Session Tags for Federated Users

Session tags allow dynamic metadata to be passed from the IdP to AWS during role assumption. These tags enable fine-grained permissions without modifying IAM policies.

Steps to Implement Session Tags

Add Tags in the SAML Assertion Include attributes in the SAML assertion:

```
<saml2:Attribute
Name="https://aws.amazon.com/SAML/Attributes/PrincipalTag:
Project">

    <saml2:AttributeValue>Development</saml2:AttributeValue
>

</saml2:Attribute>
```

Create IAM Policies Using Tags Example: Grant S3 access only if the Project tag matches Development:

```
{
  "Version": "2012-10-17",
  "Statement": [
    {
      "Effect": "Allow",
      "Action": "s3:*",
      "Resource": "arn:aws:s3:::example-bucket/*",
      "Condition": {
        "StringEquals": {
          "aws:RequestTag/Project": "Development"
        }
      }
    }
  ]
}
```

Test Configuration
   o Use the IdP to assume the role.
   o Verify permissions based on session tags.

Benefits of Session Tags

- **Dynamic Permissions:** Adjust access without updating IAM policies.
- **Scalability:** Simplify access control for large organizations.
- **Enhanced Security:** Enforce least privilege dynamically.

OpenID Connect (OIDC)

OIDC, built on OAuth 2.0, provides a lightweight federation method for web and mobile applications. It's ideal for scenarios where external IdPs (e.g., Google, Auth0) authenticate users.

Steps to Set Up OIDC Federation

1. **Register the OIDC IdP in AWS**
   o Log in to the AWS Management Console.
   o Navigate to **IAM → Identity Providers**.
   o Add an OIDC provider and specify:
      ▪ **Provider URL** (e.g., https://accounts.google.com)
      ▪ **Audience** (e.g., sts.amazonaws.com).
2. **Create an IAM Role for OIDC**
   o Go to **IAM → Roles → Create Role**.
   o Select **Web Identity** and choose the OIDC provider.
   o Attach policies for resource access.
3. **Configure the OIDC IdP**
   o In the IdP, register AWS as a client application.
   o Obtain client credentials (Client ID and Secret) to authenticate users.

4. Test OIDC Federation
- o Authenticate a user via the IdP.
- o Use the provided token to assume the IAM role in AWS.

Example OIDC Policy

Grant S3 access to users authenticated through an OIDC IdP:

```
{
  "Version": "2012-10-17",
  "Statement": [
    {
      "Effect": "Allow",
      "Action": "s3:*",
      "Resource": "arn:aws:s3:::example-bucket/*",
      "Condition": {
        "StringEquals": {
          "oidc:sub": "user-id-from-idp"
        }
      }
    }
  ]
}
```

Best Practices for Federation Protocols

1. Apply Least Privilege
- o Restrict roles to specific actions and resources.

2. Use Attribute Validation

- o Ensure attributes in SAML assertions or OIDC tokens are validated to prevent spoofing.
3. **Monitor Federated Access**
   - o Enable AWS CloudTrail to log federated role assumptions.
4. **Leverage IdP Features**
   - o Use IdP capabilities like conditional access, MFA, and user lifecycle management for added security.

Summary

Federation protocols like SAML and OIDC offer secure, scalable methods to integrate external IdPs with AWS. By setting up federation and leveraging features like session tags, organizations can simplify identity management and enforce dynamic, fine-grained access control. Combining these protocols with best practices ensures a secure and efficient identity management strategy in AWS.

Custom Identity Broker Configurations: Bridging External Identity Systems with AWS

In today's enterprise environments, integrating existing identity systems like LDAP, Active Directory, or custom databases with AWS is crucial for secure and efficient access management. Custom identity brokers make this integration possible, enabling users to authenticate using their corporate credentials while gaining access to AWS resources. This post explores the components, implementation, and best practices for building and managing custom identity brokers.

What Is a Custom Identity Broker?

A **custom identity broker** serves as a bridge between an external identity system and AWS. It enables authentication and facilitates access to AWS resources by:

- Validating user credentials against an external identity source.
- Exchanging the validated credentials for temporary AWS credentials using AWS Security Token Service (STS).
- Redirecting the authenticated user to AWS with appropriate permissions.

Key Components of a Custom Identity Broker

- **Authentication Layer**: Validates credentials using external identity sources like LDAP or custom databases.
- **STS Integration**: Interacts with AWS STS to assume roles and generate temporary credentials.
- **Role Management**: Maps external identity attributes to AWS Identity and Access Management (IAM) roles.
- **Session Management**: Issues and manages temporary session tokens for user access.

How a Custom Identity Broker Works

The workflow of a custom identity broker involves the following steps:

- **User Authentication**: Users authenticate with their corporate credentials via the broker, which validates these credentials against the identity provider (IdP).
- **Role Mapping**: Based on user attributes (e.g., groups, departments), the broker maps users to specific AWS IAM roles.

- **STS Role Assumption**: The broker calls AWS STS's AssumeRole API to obtain temporary AWS credentials.
- **Return Temporary Credentials**: The broker provides these credentials to users or applications for AWS access.
- **Access AWS Resources**: Users use the temporary credentials to perform actions within the scope of the assumed IAM role.

Steps to Implement a Custom Identity Broker

Define IAM Roles

- Create IAM roles with permissions tailored to user needs.
- Configure **trust policies** to allow the broker to assume these roles.

Example Trust Policy:

```
{
  "Version": "2012-10-17",
  "Statement": [
    {
      "Effect": "Allow",
      "Principal": {
        "Service": "sts.amazonaws.com"
      },
      "Action": "sts:AssumeRole"
    }
  ]
}
```

-

Set Up the External Identity Source

- Identify the identity system (e.g., LDAP or Active Directory).
- Ensure secure communication using protocols like LDAPS or encrypted database connections.

Build the Broker Application

Authentication

Validate user credentials against the external system:

```python
import ldap

def authenticate_user(username, password):
    server = "ldaps://ldap.example.com"
    connection = ldap.initialize(server)
    try:
        connection.simple_bind_s(f"uid={username},ou=users,dc=example,dc=com", password)
        return True
    except ldap.INVALID_CREDENTIALS:
        return False
```

Role Mapping

Map user attributes to AWS IAM roles:

```python
def map_role(user_groups):
    if "admin_group" in user_groups:
        return "arn:aws:iam::123456789012:role/AdminRole"
```

```
elif "dev_group" in user_groups:

    return "arn:aws:iam::123456789012:role/DeveloperRole"

    return "arn:aws:iam::123456789012:role/ReadOnlyRole"
```

STS Integration

Call AssumeRole using AWS SDK:

```
import boto3

def assume_role(role_arn):
    sts_client = boto3.client('sts')
    response = sts_client.assume_role(
        RoleArn=role_arn,
        RoleSessionName="SessionName"
    )
    return response['Credentials']
```

Integrate with AWS

- Pass temporary credentials to users or applications.
- Enable programmatic access using AWS CLI or SDKs.

Enhancing Security with Session Tags

Session tags allow dynamic enforcement of fine-grained access controls.

Steps to Use Session Tags

Extract attributes (e.g., department, project) during authentication.

Pass these attributes as tags in the AssumeRole **API call:**

```
response = sts_client.assume_role(
    RoleArn=role_arn,
    RoleSessionName="SessionName",
    Tags=[
        {'Key': 'Department', 'Value': 'Engineering'},
        {'Key': 'Project', 'Value': 'DevOps'}
    ]
)
```

Define IAM policies to evaluate these tags for access control:

```
{
    "Version": "2012-10-17",
    "Statement": [
        {
            "Effect": "Allow",
            "Action": "s3:*",
            "Resource": "arn:aws:s3:::example-bucket/*",
            "Condition": {
                "StringEquals": {
                    "aws:RequestTag/Department": "Engineering"
                }
            }
        }
```

```
    }
  ]
}
```

Best Practices for Custom Identity Brokers

- **Enable MFA**: Add multi-factor authentication to the external identity source.
- **Minimize Privileges**: Restrict the broker's access to required roles and permissions.
- **Monitor Activity**: Use CloudTrail for detailed logs of role assumptions.
- **Rotate Secrets**: Regularly update sensitive credentials like LDAP passwords or API keys.
- **Ensure Scalability**: Deploy the broker to handle traffic spikes, leveraging auto-scaling if necessary.

Summary

Custom identity brokers enable seamless integration between external identity systems and AWS. By carefully implementing and securing the broker, organizations can provide users with secure, dynamic, and scalable access to AWS resources. Adhering to best practices ensures that this integration not only meets operational needs but also maintains a high standard of security and reliability.

Part 4: Automation and Monitoring

Chapter 9: IAM Automation and Infrastructure-as-Code

Automating IAM with Terraform and CloudFormation

Automating IAM management with **Infrastructure-as-Code (IaC)** tools like Terraform and CloudFormation helps enforce consistency, scalability, and best practices in your AWS environment. These tools enable you to define IAM resources—such as users, roles, policies, and groups—in a declarative manner, ensuring streamlined and error-free deployment.

Best Practices for Infrastructure-as-Code (IaC) Setups

- **Use Version Control**:
  Store IaC configurations in a version control system (e.g., Git) to track changes, enable rollbacks, and maintain accountability.
- **Modularize Configurations**:
  Organize configurations into reusable modules, such as Terraform modules or CloudFormation nested stacks. For example, a module for creating IAM roles with predefined permissions.
- **Leverage Variables and Parameters**:
  Use variables (Terraform) or parameters (CloudFormation) to make configurations reusable across environments (e.g., dev, prod).
- **Enforce Least Privilege**:
  Define IAM policies with fine-grained permissions tailored to specific use cases, avoiding overly permissive policies like Action: "*".
- **Enable Policy Validation**:
  Use tools such as IAM Access Analyzer to validate

policies and avoid overly permissive access before
deployment.
- **Plan and Review Changes**:
Preview changes with terraform plan or CloudFormation
change sets before applying them.
- **Secure Sensitive Information**:
Store sensitive data (e.g., access keys, secrets) securely
using tools like AWS Secrets Manager or HashiCorp
Vault. Avoid hardcoding sensitive values in IaC
templates.
- **Automate Deployment Pipelines**:
Integrate IaC tools into CI/CD pipelines to automate
deployments and enforce consistent practices.

Automating IAM with Terraform

Terraform, with its declarative syntax and modularity, is an ideal
tool for automating IAM management in AWS.

Example: Creating an IAM Role with Terraform

Terraform Configuration File (iam_role.tf):

```
provider "aws" {
  region = "us-east-1"
}


resource "aws_iam_role" "example" {
  name = "example-role"
  assume_role_policy = jsonencode({
    Version = "2012-10-17",
    Statement = [
      {
```

```
      Effect = "Allow",
      Principal = {
        Service = "ec2.amazonaws.com"
      },
      Action = "sts:AssumeRole"
    }
  ]
})
}

resource "aws_iam_policy" "example" {
 name = "example-policy"
 policy = jsonencode({
   Version = "2012-10-17",
   Statement = [
     {
      Effect = "Allow",
      Action = [
        "s3:ListBucket",
        "s3:GetObject"
      ],
      Resource = "*"
    }
   ]
})
}
```

```
resource "aws_iam_role_policy_attachment" "example" {
  role       = aws_iam_role.example.name
  policy_arn = aws_iam_policy.example.arn
}
```

Steps to Deploy with Terraform:

Initialize the Directory:

```
terraform init
```

Plan the Changes:

```
terraform plan
```

Apply the Configuration:

```
terraform apply
```

Automating IAM with CloudFormation

CloudFormation provides a native AWS service to manage IAM resources declaratively using YAML or JSON templates.

Example: Creating an IAM Role with CloudFormation

CloudFormation Template (iam_role.yaml):

```yaml
AWSTemplateFormatVersion: "2010-09-09"
Resources:
  ExampleIAMRole:
    Type: "AWS::IAM::Role"
    Properties:
      RoleName: "example-role"
      AssumeRolePolicyDocument:
        Version: "2012-10-17"
        Statement:
          - Effect: "Allow"
            Principal:
              Service: "ec2.amazonaws.com"
            Action: "sts:AssumeRole"

  ExampleIAMPolicy:
    Type: "AWS::IAM::Policy"
    Properties:
      PolicyName: "example-policy"
      Roles:
        - Ref: "ExampleIAMRole"
      PolicyDocument:
```

```
Version: "2012-10-17"
Statement:
  - Effect: "Allow"
   Action:
     - "s3:ListBucket"
     - "s3:GetObject"
   Resource: "*"
```

Steps to Deploy with CloudFormation:

Validate the Template:

```
aws cloudformation validate-template --template-body
file://iam_role.yaml
```

Create a Stack:

```
aws cloudformation create-stack --stack-name example-stack --
template-body file://iam_role.yaml
```

Update a Stack:

```
aws cloudformation update-stack --stack-name example-stack --
template-body file://iam_role.yaml
```

Automating Policy Updates and Deployments

Automating with CI/CD Pipelines

Integrate Terraform or CloudFormation scripts into CI/CD pipelines using tools like AWS CodePipeline, Jenkins, or GitHub Actions.

Example Workflow:

1. **Push Changes**: Update IAM roles or policies in a script.
2. **Run Linter**: Validate syntax with tools like tflint.
3. **Policy Validation**: Use IAM Access Analyzer or terraform plan to verify changes.
4. **Deploy**: Apply changes with terraform apply or aws cloudformation deploy.

Dynamic Updates Using Tags

Use tags to dynamically manage access without rewriting policies. For example, tag resources with Environment or Project to control access dynamically through policies.

Monitoring and Validation

- **IAM Policy Simulator**: Test policy updates before deployment.
- **Access Analyzer**: Ensure policies are not overly permissive.

Best Practices for Policy Updates

- **Test in Sandbox Environments**: Validate changes in a non-production environment.
- **Use Policy Documents**: Store JSON policy files for version control.
- **Automate Rollbacks**: Design pipelines to revert changes if validation fails.
- **Enable Continuous Monitoring**: Use AWS Config rules to detect and prevent policy drift.

Summary

By automating IAM management with Terraform and CloudFormation, organizations can enforce consistent access control practices while reducing manual errors. Adopting modular designs, integrating IaC into CI/CD pipelines, and using validation tools ensures secure, scalable, and repeatable deployments. This approach strengthens security posture and simplifies resource management in AWS.

Chapter 10: Monitoring and Metrics for IAM

IAM Metrics with AWS CloudWatch: Enhancing IAM Monitoring and Security

AWS CloudWatch is a powerful tool for tracking metrics and logs across your AWS environment, including IAM-related activities. By integrating CloudWatch with CloudTrail, you can monitor IAM activities, detect anomalies, and automate responses to potential security threats like unauthorized role assumptions, policy changes, or root account usage.

IAM Metrics in AWS CloudWatch

IAM does not natively provide detailed metrics within CloudWatch. However, you can leverage **CloudTrail logs** to extract actionable insights and create custom metrics for IAM monitoring.

Key IAM Activities to Monitor

- **IAM Policy Changes**:
  Track modifications to user, group, or role policies. Example events: PutUserPolicy, AttachRolePolicy.
- **Role Assumption**:
  Monitor AssumeRole events to track when and how roles are used.
- **Authentication Failures**:
  Detect failed login attempts through ConsoleLogin events.
- **Root User Activity**:
  Monitor RootLogin events to identify unusual root account usage.
- **Access Key Usage**:
  Track events like CreateAccessKey and DeleteAccessKey for anomalies or unauthorized activity.

Setting Custom Alarms for IAM Anomalies

Custom alarms in CloudWatch can help detect unusual IAM activity and trigger automated responses.

1. Enable CloudTrail for IAM Logging

- **Steps**:
    1. Navigate to CloudTrail in the AWS Management Console.
    2. Create or verify a trail that logs IAM-related API calls.
    3. Configure the trail to send logs to an S3 bucket and optionally stream logs to CloudWatch Logs.

2. Create a CloudWatch Log Group

Set up a dedicated log group for IAM-related logs.

```
aws logs create-log-group --log-group-name IAMLogGroup
```

3. Define Metric Filters

Metric filters analyze CloudTrail logs and extract specific IAM activity data.

Example: Detect Root Account Usage

Filter Pattern:

```
{($.eventSource = "signin.amazonaws.com") && ($.eventName = "ConsoleLogin") && ($.userIdentity.type = "Root")}
```

CloudWatch Command:

```
aws logs put-metric-filter \
  --log-group-name IAMLogGroup \
  --filter-name RootAccountUsage \
  --filter-pattern '{($.eventSource = "signin.amazonaws.com") && ($.eventName = "ConsoleLogin") && ($.userIdentity.type = "Root")}' \
  --metric-transformations metricName=RootAccountUsage,metricNamespace=IAMActivity,metricValue=1
```

-

---

4. Create Custom Alarms

Set up alarms based on metrics extracted from CloudTrail logs.

Example: Root Account Usage Alarm

- **Steps**:
    1. Navigate to CloudWatch → Alarms → Create Alarm.
    2. Select metric: IAMActivity → RootAccountUsage.
    3. Set a threshold (e.g., ≥ 1 occurrence in a 5-minute window).
    4. Configure an action to notify via Amazon SNS or trigger a Lambda function.

Other Use Cases for IAM Alarms

Monitor Unusual Role Assumptions

Filter Pattern:

{($.eventSource = "sts.amazonaws.com") && ($.eventName = "AssumeRole")}

- **Metric Name**: RoleAssumption

Detect Unauthorized Policy Changes

Filter Pattern:

{($.eventSource = "iam.amazonaws.com") && (($.eventName = "AttachUserPolicy") || ($.eventName = "PutUserPolicy"))}

- **Metric Name**: UnauthorizedPolicyChanges

Track Failed Login Attempts

Filter Pattern:

{($.eventSource = "signin.amazonaws.com") && ($.eventName = "ConsoleLogin") && ($.responseElements.errorMessage = "Failed authentication")}

- **Metric Name**: FailedLogins

Automating Responses to IAM Anomalies

Send Notifications via SNS

Notify your security team by subscribing to an Amazon SNS topic that receives alarm alerts.

Trigger AWS Lambda Functions

Automate remediation actions for detected anomalies.

Example: Lambda Function for Root Account Usage

```python
import boto3

def lambda_handler(event, context):
    client = boto3.client('sns')
    client.publish(
        TopicArn='arn:aws:sns:us-east-1:123456789012:SecurityAlerts',
        Message='Root account login detected. Investigate immediately.',
        Subject='ALERT: Root Account Login'
    )
```

Best Practices for IAM Monitoring with CloudWatch

- **Enable CloudTrail Across All Accounts**:
  Use AWS Organizations to ensure consistent monitoring in multi-account setups.
- **Aggregate Logs Centrally**:
  Stream logs from member accounts to a central CloudWatch Log Group for better visibility.

- **Regularly Review Alarms**:
  Adjust thresholds and filters as your environment
  evolves to ensure meaningful alerts.
- **Integrate with Security Services**:
  Forward IAM activity logs to AWS Security Hub for a
  unified security view.

Summary

AWS CloudWatch, combined with CloudTrail, provides a robust
monitoring solution for IAM activities. By creating custom
metrics and alarms for key events—such as root account usage,
policy changes, and login failures—you can enhance security,
detect anomalies, and automate responses. Following best
practices ensures comprehensive monitoring and swift
remediation to maintain a strong security posture.

Monitoring Access Patterns with CloudTrail Logs

AWS CloudTrail provides a detailed record of API calls and events across your AWS environment. By analyzing these logs, you can monitor access patterns, detect anomalies, and ensure compliance with security and operational policies. Access pattern analysis offers insights into who accessed what resources, when, and how, helping to strengthen your AWS security posture.

Setting Up CloudTrail for Monitoring

Enable CloudTrail

1. Log in to the AWS Management Console.
2. Navigate to **CloudTrail** → **Trails**.
3. Create or configure a trail to capture API calls:
   - Enable **Management Events** (default) to log AWS service API calls.
   - Optionally enable **Data Events** for granular logging (e.g., S3 object-level access).
4. Store logs in an S3 bucket and optionally stream them to CloudWatch Logs for real-time monitoring.

Stream Logs to CloudWatch

1. Create or use an existing CloudWatch Log Group.
2. Configure CloudTrail to send logs to the Log Group.
3. Use CloudWatch Metrics and Filters to set up real-time alerts.

Analyzing Access Patterns

Key Metrics to Monitor

1. **Who accessed your resources?**
   - Identify users or roles initiating API calls using the userIdentity field in CloudTrail logs.
2. **What resources were accessed?**
   - Examine the requestParameters and resource fields to determine accessed resources.
3. **When and where was access attempted?**
   - Use the eventTime and sourceIPAddress fields to track time and origin of access.
4. **How were resources accessed?**
   - Analyze the eventSource (e.g., s3.amazonaws.com) and eventName (e.g., GetObject).

Example Use Cases

Access Pattern Analysis for S3 Buckets

Objective: Identify all users who downloaded objects from a specific S3 bucket.

Filter CloudTrail Logs:
Search for eventName: GetObject and eventSource: s3.amazonaws.com.

Analyze a Sample Log Entry:

```
{
  "eventTime": "2023-12-07T12:00:00Z",
```

```
"eventSource": "s3.amazonaws.com",
"eventName": "GetObject",
"userIdentity": {
    "type": "IAMUser",
    "userName": "JohnDoe"
},
"sourceIPAddress": "203.0.113.25",
"requestParameters": {
    "bucketName": "example-bucket",
    "key": "path/to/object.txt"
}
}
```

Insights:
User JohnDoe accessed path/to/object.txt in example-bucket from IP 203.0.113.25.

Root User Monitoring

Objective: Detect unauthorized root user activity.

1. **Filter CloudTrail Logs**:
   - Search for userIdentity.type: Root and sensitive events like CreateUser or UpdateAccountPasswordPolicy.
2. **Set Up Alerts**:
   - Use CloudWatch alarms to notify on root user activity.

API Usage Trends

Objective: Track API usage trends for a specific service, such as EC2.

1. **Filter CloudTrail Logs**:
   - o   Search for eventSource: ec2.amazonaws.com.
2. **Analyze Patterns**:
   - o   Identify frequent actions (e.g., StartInstances, StopInstances) and active users or roles.

Tools for Access Pattern Analysis

AWS Athena

Athena enables SQL-like querying of CloudTrail logs stored in S3.

Set Up Athena:

Define a table schema for CloudTrail logs in S3.

```
CREATE EXTERNAL TABLE cloudtrail_logs (
    eventTime string,
    eventName string,
    userIdentity struct<type:string, userName:string>,
    sourceIPAddress string,
    eventSource string,
    requestParameters string
)
```

Example Query:

Identify failed login attempts:

```
SELECT eventTime, userIdentity.userName, sourceIPAddress
FROM cloudtrail_logs
```

```
WHERE eventName = 'ConsoleLogin' AND
responseElements.errorMessage = 'Failed authentication'
```

Benefits:
Fast, ad-hoc queries with no infrastructure overhead.

Amazon Detective

Detective provides visualizations and insights into access patterns and anomalies.

1. **Enable Detective**:
   o Integrate CloudTrail and VPC Flow Logs for detailed analysis.
2. **Use Cases**:
   o Visualize IAM role assumptions and API calls.
   o Correlate unusual activity across services.

AWS CloudWatch Insights

CloudWatch Insights allows real-time and historical analysis of CloudTrail logs.

Example Query:

Find AssumeRole events:

```
fields @timestamp, eventName, userIdentity.arn,
sourceIPAddress

| filter eventName = "AssumeRole"

| sort @timestamp desc
```

Visualize Data:
Create graphs or dashboards to track trends.

Automating Access Pattern Monitoring

Set Alerts for Anomalies

- Use CloudWatch alarms to detect unusual events, such as:
    - High AssumeRole API calls.
    - Frequent failed login attempts.

Integrate with AWS Security Hub

- Consolidate findings from CloudTrail and other services for a centralized security overview.

Automate Responses with Lambda

- Trigger Lambda functions for automatic remediation.
- **Example**: Revoke session tokens for compromised users.

Best Practices for Access Pattern Monitoring

1. **Enable Multi-Region Trails**:
    - Ensure all regions are covered to avoid missing activity logs.
2. **Use Detailed Logs for Sensitive Resources**:
    - Enable data events for S3 buckets or Lambda functions with sensitive data.
3. **Review Logs Regularly**:

- o Periodically analyze logs to detect unused permissions or suspicious activity.
4. **Combine with Least Privilege**:
    - o Use access pattern analysis to refine IAM policies and enforce least privilege.

Summary

AWS CloudTrail logs offer a comprehensive view of access patterns, helping to monitor activity, detect anomalies, and ensure compliance. By leveraging tools like Athena, CloudWatch Insights, and Amazon Detective, you can gain actionable insights, automate responses, and enhance your AWS security posture. Regular analysis of access patterns is a cornerstone of maintaining a secure and well-audited AWS environment.

Automating Anomaly Detection with AWS Security Hub

AWS Security Hub centralizes security findings from various AWS services, including CloudTrail, GuardDuty, IAM Access Analyzer, and third-party tools, providing a unified view of your security posture. By leveraging automated anomaly detection, Security Hub helps identify, prioritize, and respond to potential security issues, ensuring a proactive approach to securing your AWS environment.

Setting Up AWS Security Hub

Enable Security Hub

1. Log in to the AWS Management Console.
2. Navigate to **Security Hub** → **Settings** → **Enable Security Hub**.
3. Select optional integrations:
   - **Amazon GuardDuty**: Detects threats such as unusual API activity or credential compromise.
   - **AWS Config**: Monitors compliance with security standards.
   - **Amazon Macie**: Identifies sensitive data exposure.

Multi-Account Setup

1. Use **AWS Organizations** to enable Security Hub across all member accounts.
2. Designate a **Management Account** to aggregate findings for centralized monitoring.

Configuring Automated Anomaly Detection

Key Integrations

- **CloudTrail**: Monitors API calls and detects anomalies, such as root user activity or policy changes.
- **GuardDuty**: Provides anomaly detection for threats like compromised credentials or unusual geolocations.
- **IAM Access Analyzer**: Identifies overly permissive policies and resource-sharing risks.

Built-In Security Standards

Security Hub supports automated checks against the following frameworks:

- **CIS AWS Foundations Benchmark**.
- **AWS Foundational Security Best Practices**.
- **PCI DSS (Payment Card Industry Data Security Standard)**.

Automating Detection of Common Anomalies

Root User Activity

- **Detection**: Unauthorized use of the root account.
- **Response**: Trigger SNS alerts and disable programmatic access keys for the root user.

Excessive Role Assumptions

- **Detection**: Monitor high volumes of AssumeRole API calls, which may indicate compromised credentials.
- **Response**: Use Lambda to temporarily revoke permissions.

Unusual Login Locations

- **Detection**: Use GuardDuty to flag logins from suspicious geolocations.
- **Response**: Notify the security team and enable conditional access controls.

Policy Changes

- **Detection**: Track IAM API calls like AttachRolePolicy or PutUserPolicy.
- **Response**: Forward findings to Security Hub and roll back unauthorized changes.

Automating Responses to Findings

Step 1: Configure Automated Workflows

Use CloudWatch Event Rules to respond to findings.

Example Rule: Detect findings with HIGH or CRITICAL severity:

```
{
  "source": ["aws.securityhub"],
  "detail-type": ["Security Hub Findings - Imported"],
  "detail": {
    "severity": {
      "label": ["HIGH", "CRITICAL"]
    }
  }
}
```

Step 2: Trigger AWS Lambda for Remediation

Create a Lambda function to automate anomaly responses.

Example Lambda Function: Rollback unauthorized IAM policy changes:

```python
import boto3

def lambda_handler(event, context):
    finding = event['detail']['findings'][0]
    policy_name = finding['Resources'][0]['Id']
    iam = boto3.client('iam')

    iam.delete_policy(PolicyArn=f"arn:aws:iam::123456789012:policy/{policy_name}")
    return {
        "statusCode": 200,
        "body": f"Policy {policy_name} has been deleted"
    }
```

Step 3: Notify via SNS

Configure Amazon SNS to alert your security team when critical findings are detected or Lambda actions are triggered.

Analyzing and Prioritizing Findings

Severity Levels

Security Hub categorizes findings into the following severity levels:

- **INFORMATIONAL**
- **LOW**
- **MEDIUM**
- **HIGH**
- **CRITICAL**

Focus on HIGH and CRITICAL findings for immediate resolution.

Insights

Use prebuilt and custom insights to analyze findings:

- **Example Prebuilt Insight**: IAM roles with overly permissive policies.
- **Example Custom Insight**: Findings related to S3 buckets with public access.

Query Example: S3 buckets with public access:

```
{

"Filters": {

  "ResourceType": ["S3 Bucket"],

  "ComplianceStatus": ["FAILED"]

 }

}
```

Best Practices for Automating Anomaly Detection

1. **Enable All Relevant Integrations**:
   Combine findings from GuardDuty, CloudTrail, IAM Access Analyzer, and Config for a comprehensive view.
2. **Prioritize Findings**:
   Use severity levels and compliance statuses to focus on the most critical issues.
3. **Automate Response Pipelines**:
   Use Lambda functions or third-party tools to automatically remediate critical findings.
4. **Use Suppression Rules**:
   Suppress false positives to reduce noise and focus on genuine threats.
5. **Enable Multi-Region Monitoring**:
   Aggregate findings from all AWS regions for a unified security view.

Example Workflow for Automated Anomaly Detection

1. **Detection**: GuardDuty identifies anomalous API activity and sends a finding to Security Hub.
2. **Analysis**: Security Hub aggregates the finding and evaluates its severity.
3. **Response**: CloudWatch triggers a Lambda function to remediate the issue.
4. **Notification**: An SNS alert notifies the security team of the incident and remediation actions.

Integrating Security Hub with Third-Party Tools

- **SIEM Integration**: Forward findings to tools like Splunk or Datadog for enhanced event correlation and analysis.

- **Ticketing Systems**: Create incident tickets in platforms like Jira or ServiceNow for tracking and resolution.

Summary

AWS Security Hub simplifies anomaly detection by aggregating findings from AWS services and third-party tools. Automated workflows with CloudWatch, Lambda, and SNS ensure prompt remediation of critical issues. By prioritizing findings, leveraging insights, and integrating with broader security ecosystems, organizations can maintain a secure and compliant AWS environment.

Part 5: Appendices

Glossary of AWS IAM Terms

This glossary provides definitions of key terms related to AWS Identity and Access Management (IAM), helping you understand foundational concepts and features.

A

- **Access Advisor**: A feature in IAM that shows when an IAM entity (user, role, or group) last accessed specific AWS services, helping optimize permissions.
- **Access Key**: A pair of credentials (Access Key ID and Secret Access Key) used to authenticate programmatic requests to AWS, associated with IAM users or roles.
- **AWS Organizations**: A service for centralized management of multiple AWS accounts, supporting governance through features like consolidated billing and Service Control Policies (SCPs).

C

- **Condition Key**: A key in IAM policies that refines permissions based on attributes such as time, IP address, or tags (e.g., aws:SourceIp, aws:CurrentTime).
- **Cross-Account Access**: A setup allowing users or roles in one AWS account to access resources in another account using IAM roles and trust relationships.

D

- **Data Events**: CloudTrail logs that track specific operations on resources, such as S3 object-level access (e.g., GetObject, PutObject).
- **Delegation**: Granting permissions to users or roles to act on behalf of another entity, often using IAM roles or temporary credentials.

E

- **Effect**: The directive in an IAM policy statement that determines whether access is Allow or Deny.

G

- **Group**: A collection of IAM users to which permissions can be assigned collectively using managed or inline policies.

I

- **IAM (Identity and Access Management)**: The AWS service that provides secure control over access to AWS resources by managing users, roles, groups, and policies.
- **IAM Access Analyzer**: A tool that analyzes resource-based policies to identify resources accessible publicly or cross-account.
- **Inline Policy**: A policy directly embedded within an IAM entity (user, group, or role) and not shared with others.

K

- **Key Pair**: A set of security credentials (public and private keys) used for securely connecting to Amazon EC2 instances.

L

- **Last Accessed Information**: Metadata in IAM showing when a user or role last accessed a service or resource, aiding in permission refinement.

M

- **Managed Policy**: An IAM policy that is either AWS-managed (predefined by AWS) or customer-managed (created and managed by you).
- **Multi-Factor Authentication (MFA)**: A security mechanism requiring two or more authentication factors, such as a password and a time-based OTP.

O

- **Organizational Unit (OU)**: A container within AWS Organizations used to group AWS accounts for centralized management and SCP application.

P

- **Permission Boundary**: A policy that defines the maximum permissions a user or role can have.

- **Policy**: A JSON document that defines permissions, which can be managed (AWS or customer-managed) or inline.
- **Principal**: The entity (user, role, or AWS service) allowed or denied access to a resource.

R

- **Resource**: An AWS entity such as an S3 bucket, EC2 instance, or DynamoDB table that permissions apply to in an IAM policy.
- **Role**: An IAM entity granting temporary permissions to users, applications, or AWS services.

S

- **Service Control Policy (SCP)**: A feature in AWS Organizations that defines the maximum permissions available for accounts in an organization or OU.
- **Session Tags**: Metadata passed as tags when assuming a role, enabling fine-grained access control based on dynamic attributes.
- **STS (Security Token Service)**: A service providing temporary credentials for users, roles, or applications.

T

- **Temporary Credentials**: Short-term credentials issued by AWS STS, used for authentication and access to AWS resources, often in conjunction with IAM roles.
- **Trust Policy**: A policy attached to an IAM role defining which principals can assume the role.

U

- **User**: An IAM entity representing a person or application interacting with AWS, with long-term credentials and policies attached.

V

- **Version**: The version of the IAM policy language. Current version: "2012-10-17".

Summary

This glossary provides concise definitions of IAM-related concepts and terms to help you better understand AWS identity and access management features and practices, ensuring secure and efficient management of your AWS environment.

Policy Templates for Common Scenarios

This guide provides AWS IAM policy templates for frequently encountered access management scenarios. Each template can be customized by modifying the resource ARNs, actions, or conditions to fit specific requirements.

1. Read-Only Access to S3

Scenario: Provide read-only access to all objects in a specific S3 bucket.

```
{
  "Version": "2012-10-17",
  "Statement": [
    {
      "Effect": "Allow",
      "Action": [
        "s3:GetObject",
        "s3:ListBucket"
      ],
      "Resource": [
        "arn:aws:s3:::example-bucket",
        "arn:aws:s3:::example-bucket/*"
      ]
    }
  ]
}
```

2. Full Access to EC2

Scenario: Grant full control over EC2 resources in a specific region.

```json
{
    "Version": "2012-10-17",
    "Statement": [
        {
            "Effect": "Allow",
            "Action": "ec2:*",
            "Resource": "*",
            "Condition": {
                "StringEquals": {
                    "aws:RequestedRegion": "us-east-1"
                }
            }
        }
    ]
}
```

3. Restrict Access to an S3 Bucket by IP Address

Scenario: Allow S3 access only from a specific IP range.

```json
{
    "Version": "2012-10-17",
    "Statement": [
        {
            "Effect": "Allow",
            "Action": "s3:*",
            "Resource": [
                "arn:aws:s3:::example-bucket",
                "arn:aws:s3:::example-bucket/*"
            ],
            "Condition": {
                "IpAddress": {
                    "aws:SourceIp": "203.0.113.0/24"
                }
            }
        }
    ]
}
```

4. Grant Lambda Execution Role Access

Scenario: Allow a Lambda function to write logs to CloudWatch.

```json
{
    "Version": "2012-10-17",
    "Statement": [
        {
            "Effect": "Allow",
            "Action": [
                "logs:CreateLogGroup",
                "logs:CreateLogStream",
                "logs:PutLogEvents"
            ],
            "Resource": "arn:aws:logs:*:*:*"
        }
    ]
}
```

5. MFA-Enforced Access to DynamoDB

Scenario: Require MFA for accessing a DynamoDB table.

```
{
    "Version": "2012-10-17",
    "Statement": [
        {
            "Effect": "Allow",
            "Action": "dynamodb:*",
            "Resource": "arn:aws:dynamodb:us-east-
1:123456789012:table/example-table",
            "Condition": {
                "Bool": {
                    "aws:MultiFactorAuthPresent": "true"
                }
            }
        }
    ]
}
```

6. Read-Only Access Across AWS

Scenario: Grant read-only access to all AWS services and resources.

```json
{
    "Version": "2012-10-17",
    "Statement": [
        {
            "Effect": "Allow",
            "Action": [
                "*:Describe*",
                "*:Get*",
                "*:List*"
            ],
            "Resource": "*"
        }
    ]
}
```

7. Developer Access to a Specific Project

Scenario: Grant access to resources tagged for a specific project.

```json
{
  "Version": "2012-10-17",
  "Statement": [
    {
      "Effect": "Allow",
      "Action": "*",
      "Resource": "*",
      "Condition": {
        "StringEquals": {
          "aws:ResourceTag/Project": "Development"
        }
      }
    }
  ]
}
```

8. Cross-Account Role Access

Scenario: Allow users from Account A to assume a role in Account B.

Trust Policy for Account B:

```json
{
  "Version": "2012-10-17",
  "Statement": [
    {
      "Effect": "Allow",
      "Principal": {
        "AWS": "arn:aws:iam::123456789012:root"
      },
      "Action": "sts:AssumeRole"
    }
  ]
}
```

Permissions Policy for the Role in Account B:

```
{

    "Version": "2012-10-17",

    "Statement": [

        {

            "Effect": "Allow",

            "Action": "s3:ListBucket",

            "Resource": "arn:aws:s3:::example-bucket"

        }

    ]

}
```

9. Deny All Insecure (Non-HTTPS) Requests

Scenario: Prevent access to any resource if the request is not made over HTTPS.

```
{
    "Version": "2012-10-17",
    "Statement": [
        {
            "Effect": "Deny",
            "Action": "*",
            "Resource": "*",
            "Condition": {
                "Bool": {
                    "aws:SecureTransport": "false"
                }
            }
        }
    ]
}
```

10. Enforcing Resource Tagging

Scenario: Ensure all EC2 instances have a specific tag during creation.

```json
{
  "Version": "2012-10-17",
  "Statement": [
    {
      "Effect": "Deny",
      "Action": "ec2:RunInstances",
      "Resource": "arn:aws:ec2:*:*:instance/*",
      "Condition": {
        "Null": {
          "aws:RequestTag/Environment": "true"
        }
      }
    }
  ]
}
```

Customizing These Templates

- Replace placeholders like example-bucket, 123456789012, and example-table with actual resource names or ARNs.
- Adjust actions, conditions, or regions as required by your specific use case.

Summary

These policy templates offer practical solutions for common IAM scenarios while adhering to the principle of least privilege. Tailoring these templates to your organization's requirements ensures robust access control, enhancing the security and efficiency of your AWS environment.

IAM CLI Commands Cheat Sheet

This cheat sheet provides commonly used AWS CLI commands to efficiently manage IAM resources, including users, groups, roles, policies, and MFA.

---

1. IAM Users

Create an IAM User

```
aws iam create-user --user-name <user-name>
```

Delete an IAM User

```
aws iam delete-user --user-name <user-name>
```

List All IAM Users

```
aws iam list-users
```

Attach a Managed Policy to a User

```
aws iam attach-user-policy --user-name <user-name> --policy-arn <policy-arn>
```

Detach a Managed Policy from a User

```
aws iam detach-user-policy --user-name <user-name> --policy-arn <policy-arn>
```

Add Inline Policy to a User

```
aws iam put-user-policy --user-name <user-name> --policy-
name <policy-name> --policy-document file://<policy-file>.json
```

Remove Inline Policy from a User

```
aws iam delete-user-policy --user-name <user-name> --policy-
name <policy-name>
```

2. IAM Groups

Create an IAM Group

aws iam create-group --group-name <group-name>

Delete an IAM Group

aws iam delete-group --group-name <group-name>

List All IAM Groups

aws iam list-groups

Add a User to a Group

aws iam add-user-to-group --user-name <user-name> --group-name <group-name>

Remove a User from a Group

aws iam remove-user-from-group --user-name <user-name> --group-name <group-name>

Attach a Managed Policy to a Group

aws iam attach-group-policy --group-name <group-name> --policy-arn <policy-arn>

Detach a Managed Policy from a Group

```
aws iam detach-group-policy --group-name <group-name> --
policy-arn <policy-arn>
```

3. IAM Roles

Create an IAM Role

aws iam create-role --role-name <role-name> --assume-role-policy-document file://<trust-policy>.json

Delete an IAM Role

aws iam delete-role --role-name <role-name>

Attach a Managed Policy to a Role

aws iam attach-role-policy --role-name <role-name> --policy-arn <policy-arn>

Detach a Managed Policy from a Role

aws iam detach-role-policy --role-name <role-name> --policy-arn <policy-arn>

Add Inline Policy to a Role

aws iam put-role-policy --role-name <role-name> --policy-name <policy-name> --policy-document file://<policy-file>.json

Remove Inline Policy from a Role

aws iam delete-role-policy --role-name <role-name> --policy-name <policy-name>

4. IAM Policies

List All Managed Policies

aws iam list-policies

Create a Customer-Managed Policy

aws iam create-policy --policy-name <policy-name> --policy-document file://<policy-file>.json

Delete a Customer-Managed Policy

aws iam delete-policy --policy-arn <policy-arn>

Get Policy Details

aws iam get-policy --policy-arn <policy-arn>

Get Policy Version

aws iam get-policy-version --policy-arn <policy-arn> --version-id <version-id>

5. Multi-Factor Authentication (MFA)

Enable MFA for a User

```
aws iam enable-mfa-device --user-name <user-name> --serial-
number <device-arn> --authentication-code1 <code1> --
authentication-code2 <code2>
```

Deactivate MFA for a User

```
aws iam deactivate-mfa-device --user-name <user-name> --
serial-number <device-arn>
```

List MFA Devices for a User

```
aws iam list-mfa-devices --user-name <user-name>
```

---

6. Access Keys

Create Access Keys for a User

aws iam create-access-key --user-name <user-name>

Delete Access Keys for a User

aws iam delete-access-key --user-name <user-name> --access-key-id <access-key-id>

List Access Keys for a User

aws iam list-access-keys --user-name <user-name>

Update Access Key Status

aws iam update-access-key --user-name <user-name> --access-key-id <access-key-id> --status <Active|Inactive>

---

7. Miscellaneous Commands

Get IAM User Information

```
aws iam get-user --user-name <user-name>
```

Simulate Policy Permissions

```
aws iam simulate-principal-policy --policy-source-arn <arn> --action-names <action1> <action2>
```

List Entities That Use a Policy

```
aws iam list-entities-for-policy --policy-arn <policy-arn>
```

Generate a Credential Report

```
aws iam generate-credential-report
```

Download the Credential Report

```
aws iam get-credential-report
```

Examples

Create a User and Add Them to a Group

aws iam create-user --user-name developer1

aws iam add-user-to-group --user-name developer1 --group-name Developers

Attach a Policy to a Role

aws iam attach-role-policy --role-name EC2AccessRole --policy-arn arn:aws:iam::aws:policy/AmazonEC2FullAccess

Simulate User Permissions

aws iam simulate-principal-policy --policy-source-arn arn:aws:iam::123456789012:user/developer1 --action-names s3:GetObject

---

Best Practices for IAM CLI

1. **Use Roles Instead of Long-Term Credentials**: Avoid creating access keys for IAM users when roles can be used.
2. **Avoid Using the Root Account**: Use IAM users or roles for CLI operations instead of the root account.
3. **Secure Access Keys**: Store access keys securely, rotate them periodically, and disable inactive keys.
4. **Test Policies Before Applying**: Use the simulate-principal-policy command to validate policies before applying them.

5. **Monitor Credential Reports**: Regularly generate and review credential reports to ensure compliance.

This cheat sheet simplifies IAM CLI operations, enabling efficient management of users, roles, policies, and access controls in AWS environments.

Troubleshooting Common IAM Errors

IAM errors, such as **AccessDenied** and trust policy misconfigurations, are common when managing permissions in AWS. This guide provides step-by-step solutions to identify and resolve these issues effectively.

Debugging AccessDenied Errors

The **AccessDenied** error occurs when a principal (user, role, or service) lacks the necessary permissions for an action or resource.

Common Causes

1. Missing permissions in policies attached to the principal.
2. Explicit **Deny** in an IAM policy or Service Control Policy (SCP).
3. Resource-based policy restrictions.
4. Conditions like MFA, IP restrictions, or session tags not met.

Steps to Resolve AccessDenied Errors

Understand the Error Message

Example error:

```
User: arn:aws:iam::123456789012:user/JohnDoe is not
authorized to perform: s3:ListBucket on resource:
arn:aws:s3:::example-bucket
```

Focus on the denied action (s3:ListBucket) and resource (arn:aws:s3:::example-bucket).

Simulate Permissions

Use the IAM Policy Simulator to verify if the principal's policies grant the required permissions:

```
aws iam simulate-principal-policy --policy-source-arn
arn:aws:iam::123456789012:user/JohnDoe --action-names
s3:ListBucket --resource-arns arn:aws:s3:::example-bucket
```

Review Attached Policies

Check all policies attached to the user, group, or role:

```
aws iam list-attached-user-policies --user-name JohnDoe
```

```
aws iam list-group-policies --group-name Developers
```

Check Resource-Based Policies

Verify if a resource-based policy (e.g., S3 bucket policy) restricts access:

```
aws s3api get-bucket-policy --bucket example-bucket
```

Evaluate Service Control Policies (SCPs)

If using AWS Organizations, ensure SCPs do not block required actions:

```
aws organizations list-policies --filter
SERVICE_CONTROL_POLICY
```

Verify Policy Conditions

Ensure any conditions in the policy are satisfied, such as MFA requirements:

```
"Condition": {
  "Bool": {
    "aws:MultiFactorAuthPresent": "true"
  }
}
```

Use IAM Access Analyzer
Validate whether a principal has access to the resource and identify missing permissions.

Resolving Trust Policy Misconfigurations

Trust policies define which principals can assume an IAM role. Misconfigurations can result in **AccessDenied** errors when attempting to assume a role.

Common Issues

1. Incorrect or missing **Principal** field in the trust policy.
2. Invalid trust relationships (e.g., wrong account or service).
3. Missing sts:AssumeRole permissions for the calling principal.

Steps to Fix Trust Policy Issues

Verify the Trust Policy

Retrieve the trust policy:

```
aws iam get-role --role-name ExampleRole
```

Example Trust Policy:

```
{
  "Version": "2012-10-17",
  "Statement": [
    {
      "Effect": "Allow",
      "Principal": {
        "AWS": "arn:aws:iam::123456789012:user/JohnDoe"
      },
      "Action": "sts:AssumeRole"
    }
  ]
}
```

Correct the Principal Field
Ensure the correct format for the Principal field:
- **AWS Account**: arn:aws:iam::<account-id>:root
- **IAM User/Role**: Full ARN (e.g., arn:aws:iam::123456789012:user/JohnDoe)
- **Service**: Service name (e.g., ec2.amazonaws.com).

Verify Role Assumption Permissions

Check if the caller has sts:AssumeRole permissions:

```
{

  "Effect": "Allow",

  "Action": "sts:AssumeRole",

  "Resource": "arn:aws:iam::123456789012:role/ExampleRole"

}
```

Test Role Assumption

Test role assumption using the CLI:

```
aws sts assume-role --role-arn
arn:aws:iam::123456789012:role/ExampleRole --role-session-
name TestSession
```

Validate Resource and IAM Policies
Ensure both the trust policy and attached IAM policies permit
the required actions.

Common Scenarios and Solutions

Scenario 1: AccessDenied for S3

- **Cause**: Missing bucket policy.

Fix: Add the necessary permissions to the bucket policy:

```
{
    "Effect": "Allow",
    "Principal": {
        "AWS": "arn:aws:iam::123456789012:user/JohnDoe"
    },
    "Action": "s3:ListBucket",
    "Resource": "arn:aws:s3:::example-bucket"
}
```

Scenario 2: Unable to Assume Role

- **Cause**: Missing sts:AssumeRole permission.

Fix: Grant the calling principal the necessary permission:

```
{
    "Effect": "Allow",
    "Action": "sts:AssumeRole",
    "Resource": "arn:aws:iam::123456789012:role/ExampleRole"
}
```

Scenario 3: SCP Blocking Access

- **Cause**: An SCP denies the required actions.

Fix: Update the SCP to allow the necessary actions:

```
{

"Effect": "Allow",

"Action": "s3:*",

"Resource": "*"

}
```

Best Practices to Avoid IAM Errors

1. **Follow the Principle of Least Privilege**
   Grant only the permissions required for specific tasks.
2. **Test Policies Before Deployment**
   Use simulate-principal-policy to validate policies.
3. **Enable CloudTrail**
   Monitor API calls to identify and troubleshoot permission issues.
4. **Regular Policy Audits**
   Periodically review IAM policies and trust relationships.
5. **Utilize Access Analyzer**
   Ensure resources are not publicly or overly permissively accessible.

By following these troubleshooting steps and best practices, you can efficiently resolve IAM errors, ensuring secure and seamless access management in your AWS environment.